SWEET RELEASE

JAMES DAVISON JR., PhD

SWEET

THE LAST STEP TO BLACK FREEDOM

RELEASE

Prometheus Books

59 John Glenn Drive
Amherst, New York 14228-2119

Published 2008 by Prometheus Books

Inquiries should be addressed to
Prometheus Books
59 John Glenn Drive
Amherst, New York 14228–2119
VOICE: 716–691–0133, ext. 210
FAX: 716–691–0137
WWW.PROMETHEUSBOOKS.COM

12 11 10 09 08   5 4 3 2 1

Library of Congress Cataloging-in-Publication Data

Davison, James.
    Sweet release : the last step to Black freedom / by James Davison, Jr.
        p. cm.
    Includes bibliographical references.
    ISBN 978–1–59102–558–0
    1. African Americans—Psychology. 2. African Americans—Race identity. 3. African Americans—Attitudes. 4. Self-defeating behavior—United States. 5. Problem families—United States. 6. African American families. 7. African Americans—Social conditions—1975–8. Community life—United States. I. Title.

E185.625.D385 2008
305.896'073—dc22

                                                            2007046645

Printed in the United States of America on acid-free paper

For my mothers—
Martha Lee Owens and Claire Marie Lyons—
and my fathers—
James Davison Sr., Dr. Reverend Henry H. Nichols,
and Dr. George A. Johnson.
Thank you.

CONTENTS

PART 2: MECHANISMS AND MACHINATIONS OF SELF-DEFEAT

PART 3: MESSAGES FOR THOSE MOVING FORWARD

PART 4: MESSAGES FOR THOSE BEING LEFT BEHIND

Foreword

MOVING DAY
Beyond the 'Hood

Dear 'Hood Inhabitants,

What in the world are you doing? Still waiting for some savior or some program to come to your street, knock on your door, and lift you out of your circumstances? Guess what? It ain't happening. The Advancement isn't coming to your neighborhood. You have to seek out your higher destiny. You have to want it more than you want the comfort of those things that are familiar to you. That means if you want more than the 'hood for yourself and your family, then you have to exist beyond the 'hood. You have to move out—away from the 'hood, and away from the racial and cultural isolation that is so pervasive there. What you seek is simply not in the 'hood. It never has been, and it never will be.

However, attaining your higher destiny is not a matter of simple relocation. I know more than a few persons who have packed their belongings and moved to more progressive environs, but failed to leave behind their ghetto ways. Along with their other family heirlooms, they packed their ghetto ways neatly and safely in bubble wrap, placed them in a box specially designed to transport such fragile—and I would say impractical—objects, and hand-carried them in the cab of the truck to make doubly sure no breakage or harm would come to these treasures. So despite a new living environment, they permitted their allegiance to old ways to continue to compromise any new opportunities.

Living beyond the ghetto is not merely a change of address. It is a change of soul. We must not only change our addresses, we must change our very spirits. How we look at ourselves and how we interact with others must transcend the tentacles of race that grasp continually at our psyches. This transcending of race is what we owe, if not to ourselves then to those black persons who arrived to this continent in chains and died still chained. It is our imperative and it is our obligation to free ourselves from the last chains.

Don't you get it? Those forebears—your ancestors—were reduced to nothing, no more than dark property without any rights, relations, or uniqueness of thought that any person in the Americas was bound to respect. If those days seem too far removed, then think of your grandmother. Imagine her as a little girl. Picture what she might have looked like as a youngster. Pigtails or nappy-headed, boney-kneed or a little tubby—a cute little girl in the sunshine, playing with her dolls or in a game with her friends. Can you see her? Is she smiling? Now picture that little girl's grandmother in chains. Can you see her? Does it disturb you? This imagery is not meant to infuriate you but to inspire you toward transcending.

We must now move beyond our own remaining chains, beyond the mental barriers that keep so many of us constrained in our thoughts and deeds. In order to do so we must *first* move beyond ourselves, each other, and our neighborhoods. We must break free from our enmeshment and seek that final step toward psychological freedom. Discovering that the world is so much bigger than you know, and realizing that there exist so many things that you may not even have an inkling of a thought about, are crucial steps in the progression toward psychological freedom. Breaking the chains of our minds and opening the door to your *individual* psyche is the key to our final step to freedom.

I have learned much about myself while outside the confines of my 'hood. I have traveled pretty extensively through the United States, Europe, Africa, Mexico, and India. All these places had very unique things to offer. While in Mexico I visited the Pyramids of the Sun and the Moon. These places awed me with their spirituality. I could almost feel the people who frequented these places hundreds and hundreds of years ago. As well, I found the intellect and intricacy of the culture and the people who built these shrines fascinating.

In India I saw poverty that nothing in the United States could match. It is not uncommon for thousands of persons to live under bridges and along the banks of rivers. Filthy, barely clothed street beggars with outstretched hands formed impoverished human gauntlets through the streets of the major cities. But in the same country I saw beauty and wealth that was unimaginable. Back in the day, the Moguls had some very, very serious cash. Much more than you could even imagine. While in Agra I walked beside a pavilion wall. When I cleared the wall, there stood the Taj Mahal—the most beautiful sight I have ever seen. I stood motionless, my breath taken away, for five or more minutes. That's just how stunning it is.

A full quarter mile before reaching her royal presence, the spray of water from Africa's Victoria Falls soaked my clothing. The falls is without a doubt the mightiest and most grand sight I have ever seen. Its length and breadth are amazing; millions and millions of gallons of water tumble majestically down to the gorges below. I cried half the day because such an incredible and glorious sight existed in a place from which black people were taken hundreds of years ago. I cried because I knew without a question that only a smattering of black Americans would ever see it. And I cried because I doubted that very many of us even knew it was there.

While entering one African country from another, travelers must exchange their money in order to purchase items. In Kenya, I collected my bills. On each bill was a black man, presumably the king. He wore a crown and flashed the countenance of royalty.

"You mean this is cash?!" I blurted out, smiling wider than I ever had in my lifetime.

"Yes," my puzzled guide answered.

"With this brother on it? I can spend this?"

My guide nodded back to me.

"Really?! That's too cool!"

We are all part of a human race. Travel, even within the United States, will help each of us throw off the smallness of our neighborhoods and the smallness of our interactions with the same people—week in and week out. Give it a try. Open yourselves up to the world. You will learn to respect the culture and history of all people. And, in turn, others will learn to respect your culture and history. While traveling not only did I learn about different cultures, but my world perspective was forever widened. I began to move away from the confining history of race relations in this nation. The grip of a four-hundred-year chokehold on my evolving psychological freedom began to loosen. Experiencing cultures and people beyond the 'hood initiated a transition to more global citizenship.

> This, then, is the end of his striving: to be a co-worker in the kingdom of culture, to escape both death and isolation, to husband and use his best powers and his latent genius.
> —W. E. B. Du Bois, *The Souls of Black Folk*

We must learn that the world is so much bigger and has so much more to offer than the 'hood. We must learn to take our places as global citizens, spreading ourselves and our history and culture beyond the confines of the Avenue or MLK Boulevard. We must become world citizens. But we cannot begin that process while engaged in the same things week in and week out. Going to get fish or barbeque every Friday is nice (and tasty), but there's so much more to see (and even to eat). Expand yourself. Start small. Go to Greek Town and have something different to eat—preferably something on fire.

Damn it, throw all caution to the wind. Go see a play or an opera. Puccini's *Madame Butterfly* or Leoncavallo's *Pagliacci* will make even the toughest of thugs weep like babies. These activities are not white. Art, culture, travel, and other new experiences belong to everyone. We were kept in slave pens by race profiteers of yesteryear. Do not let yourself stay penned up in the 'hood by heeding the words of the race profiteers of today. Soon you will see that the 'hood is insufficient to meet your needs and those of your family. So my suggestion is that you start gathering boxes, funds, and friends with strong backs as soon as possible for your move out of the 'hood.

Black delayers, the world is moving forward with or without you. I fear that too many of you will be left behind, on the side of the road—waving and trying to get our attention as we march forward. I want so badly for you to do what you need to do to join us on this journey and not be left behind. Moving out and away from the 'hood and its racial and cultural isolation is not a matter of *cannot*. It is the enmeshment, codependency, and inertia of *will not*. It is a passage that your forebears have already paid for. It is a passage that your children and grandchildren deserve. Take the steps. Leave the Struggle and join us in the Advancement. I'll see you there.

I got nothing but love for you.

James

PREFACE

I am a black man—born and tempered in a Philadelphia ghetto. I am also a psychologist. I help people move forward. That's what I do. *Sweet Release: The Last Step to Black Freedom* is a book written with those considerations in mind.

ACKNOWLEDGMENTS

Many persons contributed to the imagination and completion of this book. Some hailed from the lofty halls of academe, others from professional fields, and still others from lowly urine-scented subway caverns. Space permits only the listing of a few special contributors: Dr. Ernie Jarman, Mr. Milton Pittman Jr., Dr. Nancy Kenton, the homeless black man on the southbound subway platform at the Susquehanna-Dauphin Station, Ms. Pamela L. Smith Davison, Dr. Stanley L. Bowie, Ms. Marion B. Smith, Ms. Charlotte A. Smith, Mr. Yale W. Davison, Mr. Greer L. Davison, Dr. Althea Smith, Mr. James A. Morgan, and Ms. Tosca Toussaint.

I would like to especially acknowledge Ms. Melanie Thomson—who not only provided expert typing, editing, and suggestions, but endured my endless manuscript changes and served far too many times without remuneration as therapist. Thanks, kid.

Lastly, a special thank you to my editor, Ms. Peggy Deemer, whose professionalism and expertise helped fashion the manuscript into a much-improved form.

INTRODUCTION

We stand at the headwaters of a momentous time in our nation's history. At no other juncture has such an air of acceptance and inclusion been so prevalent. In every viable and imaginable sphere of human endeavor, the influence of diverse groups of people is visible. Multiculturalism is the word and spirit of the day, and is being played out throughout the entire fabric of American life. Unprecedented growth, limitless advancement, and expanding social opportunities exist for all Americans. The black middle class—a major beneficiary of these opportunities—has been expanding for decades, and continues to do so at a feverish pace. From economic advancements to Academy Awards; from social improvements to presidential politics, advancing black Americans are increasingly seen as significant and integral contributors to the vibrancy of multiculturalism in our nation.

But not all black persons are availing themselves of this modern-day New Deal. Many still identify strongly and align themselves with the long-standing constrictions of the past. Moreover, many black Americans hesitate, delay, or even refuse to grasp the brass rings of their present and future. With almost a sense of entitlement, they cite the deficits of the American Dream. They point out the system's imperfections rather than hailing its improvements. And, firmly entombed in the past, they stand as perpetual critics of the body and soul of our nation.

These delayers serve as a discredit to the past, present, and future of black Americans. Undeterred by threats of poor opportunities and chronic poverty, they forgo education, avoid responsibility, and acquiesce to criminality while denigrating themselves and other black persons. They derail the advancement locomotive for themselves and for their cohorts. Yet, despite their delay, we advancing black Americans still accord them status as brothers and sisters. We still consider them part of *us*. And, like a dysfunctional family that tolerates and enables its wayward members to bankrupt the larger unit, we remain shackled psychologically to the practices of these purportedly disenfranchised individuals, these discredits, these failures.

Sweet Release: The Last Step to Black Freedom encourages disconnection from black persons, black myths, and black traditions that impede individual and personal progress. It contends that, having attained physical freedom and political freedom, the final step of the climb up from slavery for advancing black Americans is psychological freedom. And that final step upward is a solitary and personal step—one to be taken alone, unencumbered by the black struggle, those still downtrodden, and the stifling "we"-ness of the black community. Presenting black Americans through a family systems model, *Sweet Release* brings the reader through those aspects of our personal and cultural development that foster psychological enmeshment and ultimately self-defeat. The central theme is that the time has come to unburden ourselves of those who choose defeat: to dump them—decidedly and irrevocably—in favor of improved psychological and emotional functioning. For many black Americans, the yoke of assumed kindredness with those who discredit our future, as well as our past, truly represents the last chains upon their psyches.

In part 1, traditional community styles of interaction that affect psychological freedom for black Americans are discussed. Enmeshment and codependency are inspected as culprits in compromising our ability to assert independent and healthy separation from our race peers. Without such separation, we cannot take the final step in the arduous journey from slavery to complete and absolute freedom. The chapters of part 2 chronicle how the dynamics of traditional community styles play out their dysfunction. Through our ghetto fables, unquestioned obedience to elders, orientation to the past, and overvaluation and overprotection of everything black, we tenaciously hold onto the familiarity of our myths. And, in the face of increasing opportunities to grow, expand, and heal, delay rather than advancement becomes our watchword and ultimately our psychological death knell. Part 3 addresses identity beyond the mantle of race. Black identity beyond the struggle and overcoming ourselves constitute much of the writing in this section. Lastly, part 4 suggests that in order to continue our individual and personal journeys toward psychological freedom, we must detach from black delayers and their self-handicapping behaviors. We must release ourselves and move beyond them and their dysfunction. It is now their choice: either join us on the road or be dumped, stuck in their ruts and trapped by the limitations of race.

All American citizens have been or will be affected by the specter of race in this country. Whether young or old, victim or perpetrator, fifth-generation American or newly arriving immigrant, the tentacles of race and racism reach us all. Ask the mother who has to explain to her sobbing young child why her classmates don't include her in their play. Observe the Asian American merchant in the 'hood who drops change in each customer's hand rather than touch them. Empathize with the white male who thinks the black female in the back of class is cute, but dares not approach her. Chronicle the overwhelming number of single-race churches in our nation. Witness the black student who feels unstated pressure to sit near the other black students in the cafeteria.

Racism is the beast that affects us all. All of us are its perpetrators. All of us are its victims. And all of us are tied together in its snare. We advancing black Americans have grown weary of its clench. By accepting and embracing ourselves beyond race, all Americans should benefit from our final liberating and humanizing step from slavery to freedom.

Part 1

ROOTS OF SELF-DEFEAT

The final step to freedom for black Americans has little to do with racism, prejudice, or discrimination. Shackling of the mind and spirit of the descendants of slaves has for some become an inheritance. Psychological freedom for black Americans represents our last and final step up from enslavement. The chapters of part 1 address traditional styles of interaction that affect psychological freedom for black Americans. Community enmeshment and codependency are inspected as culprits in compromising our ability to assert independent and healthy separation from our racial past. A psychohistorical model is used to explore how these styles of interaction result in a false connectedness—a pseudomutuality of sorts—that binds us together ill fittingly. Our mental chains can be more powerful than physical ones. The concepts of black advancers and delayers, and increased range and variability of behavior and thought are introduced.

Chapter 1

ENMESHMENT AND CODEPENDENCY
Just One Big Dysfunctional Family

The family—that dear octopus from whose tentacles we never quite escape, nor, in our inmost hearts, ever quite wish to.
—DODIE SMITH

Families suck! I wish they would all disappear.
—KEVIN (MACAULAY CULKIN) IN *HOME ALONE*

How did we ever come to be in such a mess? Legions of teenagers, pregnant or orchestrating their lives toward pregnancy, stroll shamelessly through our streets. Single-parent homes dominate our neighborhoods and typify the deficient rearing grounds of most of our children. Black males—little more than sperm donors—wander the streets engaged in an interminable adolescence. Record numbers of incarcerated persons languish unmotivated and irresponsibly in prison. And, above all else, countless black families struggle daily to survive neighborhoods besieged by virulent drug and gang cultures. For them, a family walk on a cool summer evening is near suicide. In so many tragic ways, it seems we are moving backward. After all the years of being held back and held down, followed by all the years of hope and promise, we still, as a people, struggle mightily with our direction.

27

I contend that it is not *we* who are struggling and moving backward. *They* are. *They* being those "other" black persons. The ones who defeat themselves. The ones who choose not to advance. The ones who bring shame to being black. *Those* black persons. You know who they are. You see them on the street everyday. Pants saggin'. Asses wigglin'. Prospects dwindlin'. Yes, *I* too am black. Just as *they* are. But *we* are not family. I am not them. They are not me. *We* are not we. To think otherwise blurs the mammoth distinctions between those black persons who chose to advance and those who chose to delay.

MAMMOTH DISTINCTIONS? BLACK PEOPLE?

The notion that mammoth distinctions exist among black people is probably a point of confusion for many people. Black individuality is a relatively new notion, and at odds with traditional and popular thought related to the history of black Americans in this nation. The term itself grates dissonantly with long-held beliefs about the nature and priorities of black people. Until very recently, all of us—even black persons—had become accustomed to the perception of black Americans as one relatively invariant group.[1] That is, a mass of black humanity: downtrodden and leveled by the experience of slavery, but moving collectively ever forward in a quest for full equality and freedom. That very perception of collectivity of thought and deed is inconsistent with any notion of mammoth distinctions. Although confusing, this inconsistency is actually a good thing. It identifies a monumental step forward in the recognition of multiple and disparate characterizations, ideologies, and futures for black Americans. This inconsistency also represents a cultural shift in American thinking. Such shifts are always followed by confusion. However, confusion this early in the book is not a good thing, particularly since we are less than two pages into the first chapter. So before proceeding any further, we need to talk. And we need to do so in a frank and earnest way.

For many urgent years, singleness of purpose and mentality characterized the breadth and depth of black Americans. At least that's what we put out there and what a keen media eagerly reported. Black Americans were, collectively, in a battle for survival. And that fact was reiterated every day in our schools, on television, and in intergroup relations. So any confusion today in reaction to the notion of mammoth distinctions is not unwarranted. It is neither a reflection of racial insensitivity by the reader nor suggestive of lack of exposure to black Americans. Black persons themselves, when presented with the same inconsistency, are truly just as confused as any other group of people.

This sense of confusion is fueled further by the significant historical commonalities that black Americans share. Our common genesis (i.e., slavery) in this nation, our common battles (i.e., emancipation, civil rights) for freedom, and our common transitions from rural to urban and from holler to 'hood are overwhelmingly suggestive of congruence between black Americans, not distinctions—especially not mammoth ones. But they do exist. And they are very important distinctions.

In very real and very fundamental ways, there are incredible differences. However, it has been our experiences with slavery and its aftermath that causes all Earth's inhabitants (especially black people) to endorse commonality and congruence. But, ironically, it has been these same experiences (or, more precisely, our reactions to them) that account for the most fundamental and enduring differences among us. Let's look, for example, at expectations for quality of life among black persons. Monumental differences in our vistas for life have long forged a "them" and "us" dichotomy for black Americans. Some of us (in reaction to difficult eras) have always seen the potential of the future and busied ourselves getting prepared. Others of us (in reaction to those same eras) have always seen only the futility of the past and readied ourselves for the next party, the next "high," or the next excuse-making opportunity. So even within the cramped house of black America, the expressive distinctions separating "them" from "us" scream out loudly over the weak murmurs of racial unanimity. We're just not listening.

Of course distinctions exist—just as they exist among white, brown, and yellow people. Where we black Americans have been confused is how the lines are drawn. We've let political times or our own emotional immaturity mislead us into enacting false dichotomies. For example, our variance has never been a matter of brothers and sisters versus Uncle Toms and sellouts. Nor has it been a matter of the revolution minded versus the black conservatives. Although such dichotomies have been widely publicized and endorsed, they do not represent an accurate portrayal of our differences. These labels are inaccurate and useless because in reality we've all been down with The Struggle: brothers, sisters, so-called Uncle Toms and conservatives, revolutionists, and bootlickers—All of us!

No one could deny that persons from each of these groups have been intent on moving ahead. You might disagree with their methods or philosophies, but more than likely all, in their own ways, have been trying to make life better for themselves, or at least for their children. All have been advancing forward and trying to reap the full benefits of the American system. No, political and social differences have never adequately defined our more meaningful distinctions. Such demarcations have never been accurate. Simply put, our variance is and has always been between those who choose to move forward (black advancers) and those who choose to wait for deliverance (black delayers).

DIFFERENT AS NIGHT AND DAY

The social and political conditions that fostered our differences have long existed in the United States. American history is replete with periods (e.g., slavery, Jim Crow, separate but equal) that contributed to thwart the progress of its black citizens. This fact is undeniable and not remotely debatable. What is debatable, however, is how particular black citizens and particular black families responded to these periods. The responses made (then and now) characterize and demarcate the line between black advancers and black delayers. It would be simple mindlessness to assert that all of us were similarly or equally affected by these periods and their threats. Character attributes such as resiliency (to repeated deterrents) and hardiness (in the face of future obstacles) contribute greatly to our individual approaches to difficult periods and threats. These attributes manifest themselves differently *between* each of us and may even be different *within* each of us in varied situations.

How each of us responds to pressure, stress, trauma, and attrition is idiosyncratic. True enough, most black Americans were under similar circumstances. But how we, as humans, individually react is affected by many factors. In essence, while our threats may have been common, our responses were not. For example, some persons may exhibit depression, feelings of isolation, and decreased self-esteem in reaction to what they perceive as uncontrollable life circumstances. They may adopt and model for their children a sense of helplessness and an inactive stance in the face of such adversity. Others, under the very same conditions, may exhibit resiliency, fortitude, and increased drive. They may redouble their efforts and likely adopt and model for their children a hopeful and active stance in the face of adversity.

We black persons are variant. We are not the same. For anyone to suggest common goals, outlooks, and heart for black Americans based simply on our common beginnings or common threats is wrong minded. Such a suggestion is reductionistic. That is, I and millions of other unique and self-defined individuals are maliciously reduced to black males and black females—primarily, fatefully, and conclusively. However, neither in thoughts nor in deeds are we all alike. We are not the same.

Consider, for a moment, that I might be a self-defined and unique individual. I know it's difficult to conceive (me being black and all), but humor me for a few mad, impetuous moments. I am me: not a representative of my race; not a leader, harbinger, trailblazer, or role model; not even one of the brothers or a keeper of the Dream, but only an individual. As an individual, I have range and variability. Those attributes have helped me evolve beyond my genesis. I grow and develop and move forward as a result. Those other black persons (you know—the ones we talked about earlier) squash individuality, range, and variability. They strive—and enjoin the rest of us to strive—to be or remain black, whatever that means. They look askance at activities that would move them beyond their genesis and their black selves. Ultimately, they are *delayers* in the succession from race matters to character matters. I and those of my ilk are *advancers*. We couldn't be any more different from black delayers. Even our watchwords attest to our lack of familial connection. They "keep it real," while we "keep on keeping on."

Without a doubt, we are *not* family. To insist we are is pathology, embedded deep in the American psyche and resistant to cure. It is our history as *black collective*—our clannishness—that causes us (and damned near everyone else on the planet) to discount our multifariousness, that is, to discount our selves beyond race. For those of us who swallow the black American family-at-large concept, it is codependence tying all of us to those supposed "family" members who rush to embrace dysfunctional behaviors. Insistence upon the black family-at-large concept has become, through racism and through our own misguidance, a cultural truism for United States society specifically and for the world in general.

THE ROLE AND ALLURE OF SURVIVAL

Historically and as a matter of necessity, black Americans struggled mightily for survival. Through the eras of slavery, emancipation, Reconstruction, Jim Crow, and civil rights, we needed to work together in order to survive our *common* physical, emotional, and psychological threats. During those times, our color (and little else) served to enact lynchings, rapes, murders, and countless indignities. Daily these atrocities were visited upon our forebears, who pulled together as best they could to weather these racial storms. However, our *common* threats are now gone. Forever gone. We just have to admit it. Any perceived remaining common threats are now more likely a reflection of black paranoia, traumatization by proxy,[2] misperception, or the myopia of heads only recently unburied from the sands of the past. Survival, for many of us, is no longer the issue. Despite the fulminations of black delayers, who would have us believe otherwise, survival is an economic and class issue, not a racial one. And through our efforts and those of our parents and grandparents, we have moved on up, never to be downtrodden again. Yet we still somehow find ourselves psychologically entrenched in survival mode and, as a result, falsely connected to each other.

The reality of the matter is that there is little reason for the majority of us to still be in survival mode. Statistically, the percentage of black Americans that are middle class or better grows steadily. So survival, at least economically, is not the issue for the majority of black Americans. Survival yesterday is simply not survival today. I believe today's survival, for many persons, is more affectation than reality. It harkens back to the familiar days of the past and the familiar struggles of our forebears. But neither statistically nor in reference to our outdated common threats is survival a primary concern for the majority of black Americans.

Perhaps today's notion of survival—so readily proffered by black delayers and race profiteers—has a more duplicitous meaning and significance for its endorsers. Obviously, it has little to do with the gathering of resources or bare subsistence. The statistics for black Americans bear that out. Closer to the truth may be that people use surviving status[3] as a means of protecting their egos. That is, as a delayer, by claiming and having my application for surviving status endorsed, I am in actuality seeking to stave off negative evaluations for my poor motivation and my poor effort to advance.

There are a number of benefits black delayers receive for adopting surviving status. First, people who are surviving likely perceive themselves as tough, strong, and resilient against the system. In their minds, they have not succumbed to the system's power— unlike those of us whom they consider to be Uncle Toms. In their minds, they have maintained. In their minds, they have demonstrated a level of fortitude that most Americans could not. That is, in the face of the system's oppressive might, they have been powerful. In their minds. These perceptions seem to serve an ego-protective function, and such delusions may be very enticing and alluring for persons who otherwise feel ineffectual beyond the 'hood.

Second, people who are surviving likely perceive themselves as more connected to black strugglers of the past than those of us who have moved beyond this status. They would simplistically argue that our forebears had to survive, and now in turn it is their time to do whatever is necessary to also survive. In essence, they have overidentified with The Struggle as part of the black experience—and now adhere to it. This seems to serve an affiliative function: that is, a black delayer "surviving" today may feel that his self-initiated lack of participation in "the system" is legitimized through his intimate connection to the *real* black struggles of yesterday. In essence, black delayers proceed through life as if they are paying homage to their struggling forebears.

Scene: TWO DELAYERS STANDING OUTSIDE
HIGH-RISE PROJECTS BUILDING TEEMING WITH
YOUNG MOTHERS AND SNOT-NOSED KIDS

Keith (grabbing crotch): Damn! Who's that?!

Albert: Man, don't trip. That's Keisha's welfare worker, Ms. Jackson.

Keith (loud enough to be overheard): Girl got a booty on her.

Albert (slapping five): Who you tellin'? I peeped that a long time ago.

Ms. Jackson: Mr. Johnson, I know you don't have the nerve to try to say something to somebody when you don't even take care of those three children you got upstairs.

Albert (waving dismissingly): Go'on get in your car Ms. Jackson. Ain't nobody tryin' to hear what you got to say.

Ms. Jackson: That's the problem. Ain't nobody trying to listen.

Albert: Naw, the problem is y'all keep talking BS. Me and my partners out here tryin' to survive. Survive! You hear me? I gotta do what I gotta do to take care of mine.

Ms. Jackson: But, you're not taking care of yours! The state's taking care of yours. They did when you was locked up, and they still doing it now. Why don't you go to school or get some training so people like me won't be all up in your family's lives?

Albert: Check this out, girlfriend. I don't know where you been, but the white man don't leave nothing out here for brothers 'cept the streets. We out here living hand to mouth. I gotta do what I gotta do to get mine. I don't have no time to go to no school or train for no career. I needs to get what I can get now. Today! Not two or three years from now. Today!

ANTECEDENTS TO FALSE CONNECTEDNESS

During those restrictive eras when black Americans were threatened or killed for any and all capricious reasons, our being forced together by race helped us to draw on each other for resources, strength, and a sense of community. We banded together. Today, however, centuries of *forced banding*—when black Americans were relegated to plantations, "nigger-towns," black bottoms, and colored sections—have given way to an era of *spontaneous banding*. This latter term refers to the practice of students, families, and even strangers gravitating toward those of similar hue. Today, unthinkingly, we remain steadfastly tied together, bracing ourselves to survive a storm whose winds have died: physically, emotionally, and psychologically enmeshed and codependent.

ENMESHMENT DEFINED

Enmeshment refers to relationships between persons, families, and groups that become overinvolved and interlaced. Enmeshed relationships are so involved that boundaries that should distinguish an individual from others are blurred. Like pieces of string knotted and reknotted, enmeshed persons are entangled over and into each other and exist as if tied intricately together. What is meaningful for the family or group becomes, through overinvolvement and overassociation, meaningful and encompassing for the individual. A sense of individuality and self-direction suffers greatly as the individual finds himself caught in the meshes of the group.

Without question, we black Americans are entangled too much in the lives of our race peers. In our minds—and in the perceptions of others—we are interlaced with other black persons. "It's a black thing," has risen from passing cliché to cultural truism. From birth to death, we permit skin color to enmesh us. We are caught in the meshes of ourselves. For example, we permit the actions of other black persons to somehow have meaning for us. How many times have you said or heard someone say, "Why'd it have to be a brother?" in response to some publicized misbehavior of a black male unknown personally to us? Or, more sweepingly, "See! That's why black people can't get ahead," in response to some self-defeating behavior committed by a black stranger on the street. Such queries and statements attest to our overinvolvement and overassociation with each other.

This tradition of banding together has enmeshed us and has had both positive and negative effects upon our community and our individual psyches. It has at once provided strength of number and purpose as well as weakness of character and spirit. For example, *forced banding* helped build a sense of community when it was most desperately needed, while *spontaneous banding* has been regressive and too often a panacea for those needing a psychological crutch. Tragically, through our tradition of banding, we have become overseers for our race. We are now our own oppressors, too often castigating those who dare not adhere to the banding philosophy and segregating ourselves from the very advancing opportunities our forebears labored for us to have. In addition, for people from other groups, our enmeshed numbers have represented at times a social and political repellent of sorts, causing them to shy away from meaningful interactions. Others often feel intimidated by the possible onslaught of hundreds, if not thousands, of "sentinels of blackness" poised to pounce on even the slightest of missteps. In our blind service to the black family at large, we stand like the terracotta warriors of the first emperor of China, however without clear enemy, purpose, or master.

CODEPENDENCE DEFINED

Codependence is similar to enmeshment in that persons are overinvolved in the relationship. However, with codependence, an important distinction exists. Codependence suggests a psychological condition or relationship. People who are codependent, are subject to manipulation and/or control by another's pathology. In essence, one of the persons in the relationship has a pathological condition (e.g., alcoholism) that contributes to control of the other. For example, lets look at Kathy and Bill, who have been married for about two years. Kathy can be at times a bit emotionally abusive, but Bill believes they might be a good couple if he could only get her to stop drinking so much. Bill has had some insecurities and poor self-confidence in the past. But Kathy gave him love when he needed it so he tolerates her abusive and self-destructive behaviors. "If only I could be a better husband, then Kathy would stop drinking and be a better wife." Bill is likely pathologically codependent. Bill tries to help his wife by hiding her alcohol, monitoring her spending at the local liquor store, and offering "plausible" explanations to friends, family, and neighbors for Kathy's behaviors. Early one morning Kathy was actually found asleep on the grass in a neighbor's backyard. Although Bill questions whether Kathy is good for him, he still remains allegiant to her.

For those of us who find ourselves tied to the pathological behaviors of black delayers, criminals, and their apologists, enmeshment and codependence strike true. If in your heart you know these discredits are wrong, but still you hang in there with them because they're *black* and *struggling*, or because they're *brothers* and *sisters*, then you are likely enmeshed and codependent. Delusional thinking is at the root of these pathological associations. While all around us black Americans are experiencing unprecedented success, enmeshed and codependent persons maintain the fixed delusion that opportunities for black Americans remain poor. And, taking advantage of our overinvolvement and overassociation, black delayers, criminals, and their apologists remain interminably black and interminably struggling. They come to wear their woefulness like a badge of courage, reticent to give it up because it confirms in their minds, and the minds of most world citizens, their *true* blackness.

ANTECEDENTS TO DELUSION

The nature of our existence in the Americas contributes greatly to our current difficulties with enmeshment and codependence. Black Americans are not inherently enmeshed and codependent. No group is. However, as with any cultural tradition, interactional pathologies may pass from one generation to the next, producing increasingly resistant strains. For black Americans, the facts of how enmeshment and codependence became cultural traditions are paramount and warrant discussion.

Prior to enslavement in the Americas,[4] there existed separation of Africans by nationality, kinship, kingdoms, and—yes—even ethnicity! However, once the transatlantic slave economy was established, all distinctions between Africans were terminated. Peoples from throughout the Slave Coast and beyond were all reduced—crushed and subjugated—to one calamitous group. This group—whether called Negroes, coloreds, niggers, shines, bush babies, or any of a host of other labels—represented a reduction; an oppressive convenience for the slavery industry. This convenience continues to affect us psychologically even today. Described as slave, darkie, or property, we were no longer Senegalese or Nigerian. Darood could no longer turn their noses up at Midgan-Madhiban, which had been the tradition between these ethnic groups for more than two hundred years. Forbidden intermarriage between Ife and Modakeke meant nothing. Centuries of caste distinctions among Igbo, Mande, and Wolof peoples were no longer recognized. In the Americas, nigger was nigger; property was property.

For enslaved black Africans and us, their descendants, traditions based upon race, not culture, were begun. And this is where our psychological journey and healing begins. Connectedness based solely on race was inflicted upon the enslaved Africans, and it continues unabated for us. Up to the very present, much of our identity as black people has been racial and is rooted in enslavement and oppression. Even our treasured and fiercely held *blackness*—born out of the racial pride and defiance of the 1960s—is a reaction to oppressive conditions. Ironically, *blackness* has been both a rallying cry and a death knell for those choosing to be all they can be—daring even to exist beyond the constrictions of color.

The significance of these psychohistorical events associated with slavery in affecting the psyche of black persons—past, present, and future—cannot be overstated. Not only did we lose our definition as Africans, but we also lost the very human birthrights of individual range and variability. Slaves could not, in their own right, entertain careers as doctors or lawyers, horse trainers or gardeners. Few of us expressed our idiosyncratic natures over the slave institution's proscriptions for us all. Our very identities—who we were, what we could become, even how we ate and worshiped—were determined and limited by those over us.

Still today—hundreds of years later—we are grappling with issues related to expression of our identities as individual black persons. In many ways, we continue to show restrictedness in our range and variability. Psychologically, those losses initiated a devastating and centuries-long assault upon the psyches of black Americans. It has been an assault that negated the multiplicity of black egos, black psyches, and black selves—multiplicities that we are only now beginning to consider and permit each other.

During our nearly five-hundred-year progression from enslaved Africans to present-day African Americans, we have been visited by myriad catastrophic and ruinous times. And our traditions have held us together—bound us as family—so that we survived those challenges. But, make no mistake: those traditions are rooted in our past enslavement and oppression. Moreover, those traditions have in most instances served to bind us together *too* tightly—made us *too* involved in the lives and futures of all black persons. As a black American family at large, we have become enmeshed, and pathologically so.

THE FAMILY CURSE

In these days of broken relationships and fractured families, it might be fair to ask why a sense of enmeshment—or, more romantically, a sense of family for black Americans—is a bad idea. After all, families are seen as good things—social vehicles through which a sense of connectedness and support is fostered. Given America's historical treatment of its black citizens, one might argue that it would be prudent to avail oneself of the attributes of a larger family. Families typically recognize their members, provide strength for weaker members, and offer direction.

However, members of families also grow and develop, and not necessarily at the same pace or time. Typically, for black Americans, those persons who grow and develop ahead of the mass are not accorded family status. To the contrary, growth and development for such persons has been too often met with derision, ridicule, and censure in reaction to their advancing a bit too quickly and a bit too independently. Oreo, Uncle Tom, and sellout are the epithets that have been reserved for such advancers. For black Americans, enmeshment and codependence are the vehicles that move the bulk of the community at too slow a pace while serving to crush the drive of the self-initiated. But, more important, members of healthy, well-functioning families grow and develop toward independence. They forge out on their own, seeking self-reliance, self-direction, and goals beyond the family's horizons. Families are the nesting grounds from which we launch ourselves. However, without development of self beyond race, they become burial grounds for advancing black individuals—where dreams and aspirations toward psychological freedom lie dormant and dying.

We are not all the same. We never were. We are not brothers and sisters. And we never will be. The sooner we recognize the fallacy of the black family at large and help disavow the world of its utility, the better will be our lives. I, for one, will not be yoked by history or melanin to bums, delayers, criminals, and other ne'er-do-wells. That's ridiculous. They have chosen their paths and I mine. Each of us, individually, must explore why we would think otherwise. What do you get out of physically, emotionally, and psychologically joining the ranks of the dysfunctional? Being down with the browns? Safety? Assuagement of guilt for being successful? Affiliation? Increased relevancy? Ready-made identity without the pain of critical self-inspection?

Without question, the most critical and pressing issue facing black Americans today is our need to become individuals—to release ourselves from our racial yokes marks the end of our centuries-long journey toward freedom. We must learn to separate—to deindividuate, as social scientists term it. We must learn to take our final step. Otherwise, our advancement and psychological freedom will forever be stagnated by those who suppose themselves related to us and thereby deserving of our attention and efforts. While they drag their feet or lay motionless like dead weight, we continue to try to uplift them. "After all," they plead, "we're your brothers and sisters. Aren't we?"

"Hell, no!" I say. Hell, no.

Chapter 2

PSYCHOLOGICAL THEORIES

The mind is its own place, and in itself can make a heaven of Hell, a hell of Heaven.
—JOHN MILTON

Very dangerous things, theories.
—DOROTHY L. SAYERS

know. There's no need to say it. You see a chapter titled "Psychological Theories" and think, "Oh, my God, here we go—I'm about to get bored to death." I know, because when I was asked to add this chapter I thought, "Oh, my God, here we go—I'm about to get bored to death." I also thought the very same thing entering my college courses. Each and every time I took a course in psychology it started off with the theories. It was torture. But I promise you that this chapter won't be anywhere near as boring or tortuous as you think. I don't know why there's so much theory in psychology. I used to sit in class thinking, "Freud, Erickson, Maslow, Rogers, Jung. Theories, theories, and more theories. Just what the heck do you people know for sure?!" Everybody's got a theory; nobody's got an answer. Class after class . . . theory after boring theory.

Later, in my academic career as a university professor, I was asked by one intrepid student why I had gone into this field in the first place if it was all theory and boring. It was then that I recalled the noble aspiration that brought me to this calling, the divine impetus that would launch me on my path to psychological truth: I wanted to meet girls. You see, at my undergraduate institution the psychology courses were packed with girls. I don't know why, but they were overrepresented in those classes. Who am I to question the ways of the universe? After only three semesters I had taken seven or eight courses in psychology (and met a bunch of girls). One day I was asked by my adviser to choose a major. My transcript said psychology all over it. So, here we are.

THE BORING PART

How we relate to ourselves and to others has been a topic for discussion and study for centuries. Scientists, philosophers, writers, even poets have attempted to address the relative importance of the needs of the group and the needs of the individual. How much weight we give to individual considerations versus group considerations is crucially important in development of psychologically balanced and healthy selves. This weighing of the relative importance of group and individual considerations has had special meaning for black Americans. Throughout much of the history of black Americans, expectations for our group and from our group have taken precedence over individual considerations. Whether through a history of immoral laws or through our community's pressures to stay black, we have been pressed to remain largely within a specified range of behaviors. Exploration and development of our individual selves

---

Scene: 1940. AN AIRFIELD IN ALABAMA

Black Potential Pilot: I've always wanted to fly. I've read every book and manual about it. I just need some hours training.
White Flight Instructor: You want to fly. Boy, are you crazy? Hell no, you can't fly. Y'all ain't smart enough to fly no way. And we damned sure ain't letting you fly one of our planes. What you better do is fly your black ass outta here. And quick!!

Scene: 2005.
TWO BLACK MEN DRIVING PAST AN AIRFIELD IN ALABAMA

Craig: I'll tell you something if you promise not to laugh.
David: Yeah, okay. What?
Craig: Ever since I was a shortie I wanted to skydive. Just to see how it feels.
David: C'mon, brother. What you trippin' on? Jumping out some perfectly good plane? You know black people don't be doin' no skydiving. That's white people mess.

---

beyond black has been typically squashed and met with everything from ridicule to death.

In the course of our lifetimes we encounter many types of people with varied interactional styles. Some are quite independent, giving group/family considerations very little weight in their daily lives. Others are acutely aware of group expectations and subject their lives almost completely to the group's demands. You see them every day. Perhaps you're one of them. But most of us fall somewhere in the middle—trying to live our lives balanced somewhere between others and self. The nature and expression of that balance is the wheel that makes us tick psychologically. How psychologically healthy or unhealthy we are is very much a reflection of our relationship with self and others.

The field of psychology has provided theories and research that help in understanding the mechanisms that affect interactional styles, and thereby psychological freedom and mental health. The theories of Sigmund Freud (ego defenses), Fritz Heider (psychology of interpersonal relations), Alfred Adler (psychology of self-esteem), Karen Horney (self-esteem maintenance), Steven Berglas and Edward E. Jones (self-handicapping), Erving Goffman (impression management), Martin Seligman (learned helplessness), and countless others help lay the foundation for understanding the psychology of the relatedness between individuals and groups. How these theories play out in our everyday lives can be quite interesting.

Attribution Theory: A Practical Example

Ten-year-old Patricia got a really good grade on a test at school today. How she believes good grades come about will be crucial in how she sees and approaches the world. Patricia might perceive, "I got a good grade because I'm so very smart." That is, her ability resulted in a positive outcome. And, consistent with her perception (social psychologists use the term *attribution*), she might reasonably expect other positive outcomes will result for her life. In Patricia's view of the world and self, more good grades, successful career, nice home, and the respect of others are attainable and subject to her control. Patricia might crow, "The sky's the limit because I have the ability!"

Patricia's eleven-year-old brother, Patrick, also got a really good grade on his test at school today. He got the good grade because this time he tried. His parents and teachers constantly encourage Patrick to do his best. A thousand times he's heard, "Patrick, you have the ability, but sometimes you try and sometimes you don't." Patrick might perceive, "I got a good grade because I tried this time." That is, his effort resulted in his positive outcome. And, consistent with his perception, he might reasonably expect other positive outcomes will result for his life. But Patrick should also anticipate some negative outcomes based on times when he is unmotivated. In Patrick's view of the world and self, more good grades, successful career, nice home, and the respect of others are attainable but are dependent upon the effort he puts forth. Patrick might weigh, "The sky's the limit only if I want it to be!"

Across town live Patricia and Patrick's cousins, Charlotte and Charles. Charlotte got a really good grade on her test at school today. However, everyone in Charlotte's class got a good grade. It seems her teacher is known for giving pretty easy tests, so everyone gets a good grade. Charlotte might perceive, "I got a good grade not because I'm so very smart or because I tried, but because everyone else got a good grade too." It was just the situation that resulted in her positive outcome. She might reasonably expect her outcomes to vary, but not upon anything internal to her. Rather, the way of the world accounts for her outcomes. "What happens to me has nothing to do with my ability or effort," Charlotte might think. "It is just what the world has out there for me. It doesn't really matter what I do. The situation will determine my out-come." In Charlotte's view of the world and self, more good grades, successful career, nice home, and the respect of others are out of her hands and in some way predetermined. Charlotte might lament, "The sky's the limit, but there's also no limit to the abyss!"

Charlotte's brother, Charles, also got a really good grade on his test at school today. He doesn't know how he got the good grade, he just got it. Some-times good things happen to him, sometimes they don't. "Never look a gift horse in the mouth" is his outlook. Take the grade and run. Charles might per-ceive, "I got a good grade because I was fortunate this time." That is, luck resulted in his positive outcome. And, consistent with his perception, he might reasonably expect that any and all outcomes occur by happenstance. In Charles's view of the world and self, more good grades, successful career, nice home, and the respect of others are out of his hands and in some way random. Charles might despair, "The sky's the limit, but my getting there is just the luck of the draw!"

People often adopt attributional styles that reflect how they proceed through their lives. Those who make internal attributions, whether stable (ability) or unstable (effort), are more likely to approach their lives with vigor and resolve. They meet life's challenges with self-determination. Their credo— "What happens to me will be determined by me"—captures their sense of potency. In contrast, those who make external attributions, whether stable (sit-uation) or unstable (luck), are less likely to approach their lives with the same level of vigor and resolve. They meet life's challenges with resignation. Their credo—"What happens to me is determined by forces outside of me"— captures their sense of impotency. Such persons are likely to accept their station in life or delay action while awaiting rescue.

Awareness of such individual differences (i.e., attributional style) goes far in understanding why some of us act as black advancers while others as black delayers. Think about it. Most of us come from roughly the same historical tra-dition. Our genesis in the United States is slavery. However, the attributional styles of our forebears and ourselves help determine our economic, psycholog-ical, and emotional lot. In essence, we are not one family with the same values and outlooks; we are a multitude of families and individuals whose variations in attributional styles contribute triumphantly or tragically to our place in America.

Piaget's Theory of Intellectual Growth: A Practical Example

Anyone who has spent any time at all around little kids will recognize Jean Piaget's notions of *schema*, *assimilation*, and *accommodation*. Johnny's dad comes home with a new toy for his young son. He rolls it up to Johnny and says, "Ball." The kid looks quizzically at the object and, after a few attempts, blurts out: "Ball!" His parents are overjoyed. Their child—to them an unbridled genius—knows what the new object is. They telephone Johnny's grandparents and make them listen—sometimes for hours—to their grandson saying, "Ball!" "Ball!" "Ball!" The parents are happy, Johnny is pleased that he is pleasing others, and his grandparents are thinking graduate school.

The next morning, Johnny's mom is slicing oranges for juice. Johnny looks over at his mom. With his little chubby baby fingers, Johnny points to the oranges. Guess what he says? That's right! He says, "Ball!" "Ball!" "Ball!" Johnny at this young age has developed a *scheme* for his world. That is, all things round are "Ball." Everything he encounters that is round and unfamiliar to him is made to fit into his existing knowledge base. Things are *assimilated* into what he already knows. Later he learns that everything round is not a ball. Oranges, moons, suns, and wheels have roundness, but not ball-ness. Johnny learns to *accommodate* for these other round objects. In essence, he learns to expand his schema and worldview.

In order for Johnny to expand his world and develop, he must learn to accommodate. Similarly, accommodation (or adaptation) to new ways of existence and perception of the world for black Americans must be mastered to ensure expansion and development. We must learn to expand ourselves beyond race. As well, we must expand our perceptions of the world beyond the myopic view offered through the lens of race. Otherwise, we are left to say, "Ball!" "Ball!" "Ball!" in response to new and emerging themes of social interaction. Our schema: "Prejudice!" "Racism!" "Discrimination!" serve to keep some of us as limited and psychologically unsophisticated as was Johnny. Come on, black people. You can do it. You can *accommodate*. Johnny did!

Operant Conditioning: A Practical Example

We learn of ourselves and our worlds through a process called conditioning.[1] Put simply, we receive benefits (reinforcement) for exhibiting and repeating certain behaviors. You made your bed as a child because you either wanted the reinforcement (e.g., allowance, praise, even a smile from Mom) or wanted to avoid the consequence of not making the bed (e.g., less allowance, spanking, even Mom's disappointment). Generally, the more we exhibit certain behaviors, the more reinforcement we receive. Whether the reinforcement is cash, attention, or being perceived as a black person true to the community is immaterial. That the reinforcement causes us to repeat the behavior or causes us to hesitate at the performance of competing behaviors is paramount.

Let's look at an example of how reinforcement theory plays out in the 'hood.

Adam, a young man from the East Side, is considering attending college next year. He's very bright and everyone expects him to do well. But Adam remains a bit undecided and perplexed. He's been accepted to several prestigious universities, some on a full ride. But something unseen tugs at Adam. At first he thought it was the prospect of leaving his mother alone at home with the kids that bothered him. But uncles and neighbors would keep her safe and supported. Then he thought it was the idea of moving so far away from Vanessa, his girlfriend of four years, that bothered him. After all, the girl has a body on her and seems too easily swayed by the machinations of the homies. But they had promised each other to write weekly and visit monthly. As Adam surveys the neighborhood through his bedroom window, which is way too small to provide adequate ventilation during the summer months, it hits him. As bizarre as it sounds, and after all the work and sacrifice of his young life, Adam isn't sure he can be away from the familiarity of the 'hood. In spite of all his childhood promises to escape, become a man, and pursue a career, the neighborhood, its denizens, even its dangers afford him comfort through familiarity. This 'hood is what he knows. College? That is another matter. That is scary. New people with strange new ways in a different new setting. That would be hard to adjust to. Adam has become conditioned to the 'hood and its familiar patterns of reinforcement.

The prospect of venturing into another world and attempting to be successful there would be quite a bit unnerving. The streets were home—physically, emotionally, and psychologically. Yes, Adam could come back with a degree and a career and as a man, but he'd be a foreigner to the 'hood—transformed from one of its insignificant accouterments to one of its significant but marginalized success stories. In his young mind, he'd lose his black membership card and the meager but fiercely defended privileges it provides. Now, as regards his future, choices that should not have to be made will have to be made. Affiliation or success? Acceptance or rejection? Black or who knows?

In-Role and Out-of-Role Behavior: A Practical Example

Joni, a girl from 'round the way, finds that as she grows older people have expectations for her as a homegirl and as a black woman. When she acts in ways consistent with others' expectations, she is considered *in role*. That is, Joni's behavior is consistent with group norms and does not represent a threat to group members.[2]

However, if Joni engages in acts that are unexpected, unapproved, and unsanctioned by the group, she may be considered *out of role*. As one might imagine, being *in role* or *out of role* results in significantly different outcomes for the actor. *In-role* actors are more likely positively reinforced for their acts. After all, they have opted to fit in and not challenge group norms. *Out-of-role* actors, on the other hand, are more likely punished for their acts. Ostracization and criticism are the outcomes they receive for their acts. Black delayers fit quite nicely and comfortably as in-role actors. By definition, they remain well within the bounds of what is considered *black*. Irrespective of how we define the bounds of what is considered black, there are nonetheless boundaries imposed by perceived group norms. If Joni wants to move ahead and be more, she will have to act out of role in reference to group norms. She must become an advancer. Black advancers probably are more likely out-of-role actors, challenging and extending the range of *black*.

As regards psychological growth and development for black Americans, a number of questions must be answered. Do we make internal or external attributions regarding our success/failure possibilities? Do we assimilate or accommodate regarding our view and interaction with the world? Do we act in role or out of role as we make overtures toward self-definition? The answers to these questions either define an intergenerational journey toward psychological freedom or mark cultural hazards toward continued group enmeshment and codependency.

Chapter 3

DON'T I KNOW YOU FROM EVERYWHERE?

Pseudomutuality

There is a limit to the legitimate interference of collective opinion with individual independence: and to find that limit, and to maintain it against encroachment is as indispensable to a good condition of human affairs, as protection against political despotism.
—JOHN STUART MILL

We're all in this together—by ourselves.
—LILY TOMLIN

Why we black Americans came to act as an enmeshed and codependent group has its historical antecedents. These have been stated and are fairly obvious. However, the reason we persist at presenting ourselves as such a group is somewhat obscured. We know damned well that we are unrelated to each other. We know it and so do others. I suppose one could argue there are economic and political reasons to remain connected. But for what reason is there psychological connection through enmeshment and codependency?

It is not uncommon for humans jointly engaged in struggle or crisis or trauma to become psychologically connected to each other. From team athletes attempting to vanquish a superior team to abused children trying to survive physically abusive parents to hostages during a bank robbery, humans connect

---

**Scene: 1845. THE RAWLINGS PLANTATION—
JUNE 19—ABOUT 3:15 PM**

Abraham: It's time we gets our freedom. Tonight we takes over this here plantation!

Joshua: I don't wants me no trouble. No sir! Master Adams ain't been that much too bad to us.

Abraham: We slaves, Joshua! Slaves. I wants me my freedom! And I'm ready to take it.

Joshua: I wants freedom, too. Five more years and I'm gonna buy me my freedom like Master Adams sez we can.

Abraham: The White Man don't need to do nothing to us. We ain't never gonna get nowheres if we don't learn to stay together.

---

during critical times. And, we black Americans have had critical times. We have been at war; embroiled in our nation's most protracted conflict. This war has had particularly damaging effects upon the souls of its combatants. In length of history and depth of reach into our souls, this war has exacted a devastating psychological toll. For more than four centuries, we black people have fought a war for freedom. Battles for emancipation, battles for civil rights, and battles for civil liberties have dominated social discourse between black Americans and the rest of the world. Now, finally at war's end, we find ourselves poised at the threshold of complete and comprehensive black freedom. But here, we hesitate, unwilling to break ranks and to relinquish our greatest safety net—unity.

Early in the war we learned that to fight effectively, unity was paramount. Unity of purpose and deed among black Americans became a highly valued resource during those centuries of conflict. So we learned to close ranks. There was little choice to do otherwise. Very rarely would respect and rights be accorded to any black person singularly. Only through group cohesion could battles be effectively waged toward change. Although we found ourselves typically outgunned on many fronts, the sheer enormity of our numbers served us well. By invoking our collective numbers, collective anger, and collective economic power, our forebears pushed for victories in many arenas. And they triumphed!

That was yesterday. Today, with larger collective battles for human rights and racial respect won, black Americans should now be turning to smaller, individual, and personal skirmishes. Instead of sacrificing inestimable portions of our lives and psyches to The Struggle, we should be turning to battles that are idiosyncratic to our own individual and personal goals. In essence, nurturing and developing our *individual* selves, pursuing our *individual* senses of freedom, and relishing newfound opportunities to live psychologically healthy lives. This would seem the next logical step after victories in our *common* battles. However, in many ways, black Americans, our fellow citizens, and the world at large still anticipate unity of opinions, strategies, and goals. Some still anticipate a unified battle force, suggesting that we black Americans still share important mutual goals. We ourselves are guilty of contributing to this fallacy. A misguided presumption of mutuality keeps us tied to the larger battlefield: neglecting our personal skirmishes, fighting battles already won, and awaiting blind and lame stragglers to realize victory's arrival. I suppose that after so many disempowered generations, the opportunity to advance "a force to be reckoned with" attitude is, for many individuals, psychologically empowering. Nevertheless, the notion that there continues to exist for black Americans a mutuality of opinions, outlooks, and goals is ludicrous, and it constitutes a significant hindrance in our progression. It suggests that little variability exists within our group: one mind, one goal, one future. And, as such, a false sharedness—a pseudomutuality—is assumed. Pseudomutuality[1] advances a simplistic philosophy about race. It is a philosophy that casts the world as dichotomous in order to magnify group discord. Black and white, slave and free, and stuck and advancing are ideas that emanate from our oppressive past. Such ideas have been proffered by both racists interested in subjugation and social activists interested in liberation. That discordant groups can reach such philosophical harmony speaks greatly to the power of the notion.

Today's endorsement of pseudomutuality (aka the black experience) forwards a terribly false and tragic notion: that is, we are tied together—all of us—by our mutual black experience. We are it. It is us. And we are all related—in essence, yoked to a family of color. Pseudomutuality—damnable and crude—causes us to assume that we cannot move beyond race, that we cannot transcend its connotations. That connectedness and identity by race will always be more important for black Americans than awareness and full realization of self. What a sad, sad shame.

OUTSIDE THE BOX

For our part, we black Americans have pushed a *black* viewpoint. We've lamented the *Negro* problem. Worst of all, we've excluded others by exhorting, "It's a *black* thing."[2] And that history of pushing, lamenting, and excluding others has thwarted our individual black freedom and psychological health. At the same time, that history has given life to the black experience. Without a doubt, group concerns have too far and too long overshadowed individual concerns for black Americans.

Prior to our emancipation, there was no "black experience." At least, not one anyone thought worthy of discussion and ennoblement. Hard labor was our experience. Early death was our experience. Cruelty, debasement, rape, and lynching were our experiences. Only relatively recently have we become prideful enough to embrace a black experience flavored by more than the experience of labor and pain.

As regards psychological freedom, our touting of *black* viewpoints is troublesome. It presumes that everyone who is black feels, thinks, and aspires similarly. At least that's what the larger society and our leaders would have us believe. (You know—"It's a black thing.") Unity of purpose and deed has been of enormous historical significance for black Americans. However, historical significance does not translate rightly or justly into perpetual utility. For today's descendants of slaves and sharecroppers, unity of black souls has outlived its usefulness and serves now only to hamper individual advancement, freedom, and psychological health. When you really think about it, do black people who casually or rarely interact with you *really* know you, your opinions,

Scene: PICK A 'HOOD; ANY 'HOOD AT ALL

T-Bone: You ain't fina go outside wearing that shirt are you?
Stacey: Yeah. Why not? What's wrong with it?
T-Bone: Dude, it's red! This here's Crip!
Stacey: We don't play that stupid stuff out here. Ain't nobody
    'bout to shoot you over no color. That's just dumb.
T-Bone: So you disrespectin' my set?
Stacey: I'm saying we don't do that punk ass stuff out here.

your goals? The question seems silly to ask. Of course they don't know you. How could they? Most times, many of us barely know ourselves. So what motivates us to proffer still the notion of black ideas, black experiences, and black knowledge that we all share? I say it is pure, unbridled romanticism, at best.

Some critics would counter that it is not melanin per se that fosters a sense of mutuality but a history of common past pathways. That is, having roots in the 'hood levels us all. But even the 'hood varies.

The 'hood can be very different depending where you are reared. Recently, I had occasion to travel to Los Angeles. While there, I took the opportunity to drive through Compton—an area that has received much recent attention from the media and rap artists. It is not my intention to fuel further the East Coast/West Coast rivalry, but as compared to my experiences in North Philadelphia, people in Compton are living well. Single-family dwellings, good weather, and regular police patrols are the rule rather than the exception. Like in Philadelphia, people in Compton have bars on their windows and doors to deter robberies. And like in Philadelphia, people in Compton must deal with a drug culture and chronic apathy among their neighbors. However, there exist wide, varied, and significant differences in how people live. For example, if two young black men from North Philadelphia have a dispute, they are likely to settle it man to man, or maybe include their boys in the fray if there's some punk in them. I believe and trust that it is fairly unlikely they would get into a car and shoot into a dude's Momma's house. Thus, even when one considers the 'hood as representing authentic black experiences, little mutuality of ideas, conflict resolution, child-rearing practices, et cetera exists. Indeed, the differences among us extend to all arenas of human interaction.

So, my message to all those black delayers who would level me: *You do not know me! I do not know you. Our experiences are not shared. I am striving forward; you are mired in a bog of self-defeat. How you and your family address problems of racism or discrimination are not the same as my family does. The ways I teach and rear my children are different than yours are. My outlook and yours don't match. Despite black skin, you do not know me!!*

We must realize that mutuality is not to our individual or collective benefit, but to the benefit of those who desire to keep us struggling, questioning, and not advancing. And if you insist on considering me and other black folk as part of your family, then you have to admit that you're doing an exceedingly poor job of watching out for us. For my part, I hereby release you of the burden of *my* weight. I'll take care of myself. And I suggest that you, in your efforts toward psychological freedom, take care of your own self. Stop burdening yourself and infantilizing others. Be psychologically healthy. You'll like it.

Some readers will view these writings as the rantings of a black man who has lost his way—the ravings of an individual ashamed of his heritage and desirous to negate and separate himself from the painful history of race relations in this country. I know. I've heard the rhetoric before. I just don't accept it for two reasons. First, my heritage is not one of overinclusivity. My forebears were scholars and adventurers, daring and brave men and women who built kingdoms, sailed oceans, taught the world, and in the dead of night learned to read, avoid captors, and move north toward unseen and uncertain futures. They were strong, intrepid people not content to maintain the status quo. Second, one cannot through any means separate oneself from the pains of the past. Such reminders are upon us daily. Through our interactions with others, they strike us repeatedly. No amount of free thought, writing, or disavowal will lessen the blows of the past. The critical question for persons who push mutuality is: Having already been victimized by history, are you now willing to further victimize and hinder others and yourselves?

The continued push toward mutuality is without question the most insidious idea working against eventual and complete freedom for black Americans. More than racism, discrimination, or prejudice, pseudomutuality is the chain that impedes our completion of the final step to freedom. Insistence on our connectedness holds us back; it keeps black Americans in psychological lock-step with each other and disinclined to move forward and away from those who choose to not advance. Moreover, its false potency is foisted upon *all* Americans by people who seek some sort of advantage through fostering, maintaining, and perpetuating its existence. They profit in some illicit way by pushing the idea of a collectivity of black Americans poised against others. Race profiteers in every negative sense of the term, their gains are ill gotten. Their very existence is disturbing because they represent a perpetual rampart against racial harmony. The worse among them fraudulently offer a false bridge (e.g., increased funding to their ill-conceived programs, reparations) to racial reconciliation, a bridge whose toll is collected and recollected but never, ever, in their minds, paid in full. They use us as their fodder. We are their stock in trade.

I, for one, am tired of it.

NOTES

CHAPTER 1: ENMESHMENT AND CODEPENDENCY: JUST ONE BIG DYSFUNCTIONAL FAMILY

1. This perception, rooted in the slavery era, has had multiple political ramifications, ranging from galvanizing people toward nonviolent pursuit of common goals to eliciting fear of violent insurrection in response to an oppressive past.

2. *Traumatization by proxy* refers to the inclination of people to accept as their own the traumas experienced by their forebears. For example, although none of us were alive during enslavement, many of us live our lives as if we were directly affected by this period and institution. Moreover, such persons are apt to use any period—Reconstruction, Jim Crow, civil rights—to enact their supposed trauma and maintain their delay.

3. Interestingly, those folks who are chronically surviving never seem quite motivated to actually approach or attain the status of survivor. Attainment of that status would imply that difficult periods have been *survived* and now they are ready to move forward to more productive times characterized by accountability and self-directedness.

4. Enslavement existed well before the introduction of black slaves into the Americas. In fact, slavery dates back to ancient civilizations. For example, slavery was well established within the Mediterranean region. Arab, Turkish, and especially Slavic peoples were enslaved on a huge scale. Indeed, the word *slavery* is derived from *Slavic*, and included Caucasian, Slovak, Slovene, Polish, Bulgarian, Russian, Serbo-Croatian, and Ukrainian people.

CHAPTER 2: PSYCHOLOGICAL THEORIES

1. Many of my colleagues would disagree vehemently about the nature and basis of learning in humans. They would cite theories of social learning and modeling. To be fair, I must mention these alternate theories of learning. Now mentioned, back to truth.

2. Threat here is conceptualized as any act that may cause group members to question the relative value of affiliation versus nonaffiliation. By engaging in out-of-role behavior, the actor calls into question his or her belongingness (i.e., blackness) to the group as well as the value of group membership itself for others.

CHAPTER 3: DON'T I KNOW YOU FROM EVERYWHERE? PSEUDOMUTUALITY

1. The term *pseudomutuality* is associated with the study of small group behavior and family dynamics. Several researchers, including Wynne, Rycoff, Day, and Hirsch (1958); Laing and Cooper (1964); Laing (1967); Orwell (1946); and, more recently, Gustafson and his colleagues have studied in this area. The present use is only peripherally related to those research efforts.

2. More recently, black Americans have spoken of a nappy perspective. I, for one, hold some hope for this latest affectation of black culture. Nappy-headedness as a perspective may constitute a demarcation suggestive of varied and differing black opinions. For this possibility alone, I am hopeful for us and the rest of America. Besides, I am old enough to remember "good hair" and "nappy hair."

SUGGESTED READING

Beattie, Melody. *Beyond Codependency: And Getting Better All the Time*. New York: HarperCollins, 1989.

Cudney, Milton R., and Robert Earl Hardy. *Self-Defeating Behaviors: Free Yourself from the Habits, Compulsions, Feelings, and Attitudes That Hold You Back*. San Francisco: HarperSanFrancisco, 1991.

Katz, Stan J. *The Codependency Conspiracy: How to Break the Recovery Habit and Take Charge of Your Life*. New York: Warner Books, 1991.

Klein, Stephen B. *Learning: Principles and Applications*. New York: McGraw-Hill, 1997.

Lefrancois, Guy R. *Psychological Theories and Human Learning*. Monterey, CA: Brooks/Cole, 1982.

Lloyd, Roseann, and Merle A. Fossum. *True Selves: Twelve Step Recovery from Codependency*. New York: HarperCollins, 1991.

McWhorter, John H. *Losing the Race: Self-Sabotage in Black America*. New York: Perennial, 2001.

Sills, Judith. *Excess Baggage: Getting Out of Your Own Way*. New York: Viking, 1993.

Swann, William B. *Self-Traps: The Elusive Quest for Higher Self-Esteem*. New York: Freeman, 1996.

Weiner, Bernard. *An Attributional Theory of Motivation and Emotion*. New York: Springer-Verlag, 1986.

Part 2

MECHANISMS AND MACHINATIONS OF SELF-DEFEAT

Many of us find ourselves chronically engaged in behaviors that keep us from advancing. Rationalization, denial, and deluding ourselves and others with "It's a black thing" chronicles our defensiveness toward any perceived threat of change. The chapters of part 2 address not only dysfunctional styles of interaction, but also the ways we maintain their existence. Through our ghetto fables, through our orientation to the past, and through our overvaluation of everything black, we tenaciously hold onto dysfunctional styles of interaction.

For example, we complain about conditions and things working against us, but many of us do very little to challenge those who sell the black propaganda that perpetuates motivational inertia and lethargy in our communities. Rather, we *wait*: for reparations, for our forty acres and a mule, or for the next savior while selling the idea of our helplessness. In the face of increasing opportunities to grow, expand, and heal, *delay* rather than *advancement* becomes our watchword—and ultimately our psychological death knell.

Chapter 4

GHETTO FABLES
Aesop Ain't Got Nothing on Us

The block of granite which was an obstacle in the path of the weak becomes
a steppingstone in the path of the strong.
—THOMAS CARLYLE

Self-pity is a death that has no resurrection, a sinkhole from which no res-
cuing hand can drag you because you have *chosen* to sink.
—ELIZABETH ELLIOT

Historically, a major source of identity for black Americans has been
our intimate relationship with adversity. Over centuries, trials and
tribulations became too well known to us. The Struggle became, for the overwhelming majority of black Americans, our beating heart, our lifeblood, and
our marrow. Sadly, after so many generations of struggle, many of us continue
to define and validate ourselves—and others—through tales of adversity and
sacrifice. Barriers surmounted, obstacles conquered, and mountaintops
reached have become for us part of a psychological heritage. And the
recounting of our personal and family tales of adversity serves to establish and
animate our black identity. Our tales are told and retold and then bequeathed
like heirlooms to new generations of black storytellers.

WE WASN'T JUST POOR. WE WAS PO'.

Tales of the journey from the agrarian South to the teeming northern ghettos abound in black families and black community identity. Having attained physical freedom decades before, these tales chronicle efforts to overcome adversity in the progression toward political and psychological freedom. After all, very few black persons were free and self-directed during the enslavement era. We had yet to build and establish traditions for success and failure. As freedom's challenges increasingly presented themselves, black Americans were put to the test of addressing new and different levels of adversity. Our responses—some good, some poor—resulted in divergence for our communities: a divergence marked by hard work or by hard hustle.

A PARTING OF WAYS

A significant split in black consciousness evidenced itself after emancipation and during the Great Migration.[1] Advancers—industrious, hardworking, and up to freedom's challenges—taught their children life lessons based on venturing into the system and gradual advancement. Delayers—entitled, negative, and self-defeated in reference to freedom's challenges—taught their children life lessons based on hedonistic immediacy and waiting on the system's beneficence. Advancers became the squares and lames of our communities. For them, the 'hood was temporary lodging while working toward more appropriate digs. Delayers became the hustlers and hip folks of our communities. For them, the 'hood was—and still is—haven, sanctuary for their self-destructive and ruinous behaviors.

This historic split also resulted in a significant divergence of our tales. Advancers chronicled initial difficulties settling into the cities while setting tones of advancement for future generations. Delayers also chronicled their difficulties, but devised tales impregnated with rationalization for their lack of advancement. These latter tales became our ghetto fables: fictitious narratives of insurmountable barriers and unconquerable obstacles.

THE WHITE MAN CONTROLS EVERYTHING.

So let's agree right here to discard the romanticism of our common root black tale of positive intergenerational advancement. You know: Great-grandmother and Great-grandfather worked together in the fields in order for Grandfather (then a mere lad of twelve years of age) to have enough money for the dusty, crowded bus ride north. Then Grandfather met Grandmother at a church social, and they were married two years later. They brought Mother into the world and now here you are: the latest inheritor and guardian of the family's destiny. Although such tales are true for some of us, they are certainly not true for all of us. Some black folks were trifling right from the start, and they taught their trifling ways to their children and established trifling traditions for future generations. Whether criminals or parasites, these delayers used the black community for their own means either as shelter or as grist for their criminal and parasitic mills. They told—and still tell—fables of how the white man gave them no opportunities but as delayers. They lamented—and still lament—their lack of access to the system. On the surface their fables appeared consistent with adversity. But their fables were not—and still are not—ones of challenging and overcoming adversity, but rather of resignation and defeat. Delayers just talk more of adversity so that they might rationalize their delay, their criminality, and their parasitic existence.

Other black folks chose to work in the system. They worked hard and taught their children traditions based on diligence and progression through the system. They too lamented lack of access, but they chose to redouble their efforts in the face of adversity. Perseverance and integrity became their watchwords.

WE WERE BROUGHT HERE IN CHAINS.

Thus, two separate histories of traditions, storytelling, and ultimately lifestyles were begun in the post-emancipation period. One must remember traditions based on centuries of African life had been destroyed and were now being replaced by new traditions born of oppression. In the postenslavement era, black Americans became separated not by culture or geography, but by resiliency to adversity.

Tales of adversity became either floor or ceiling in black consciousness. For delayers, adversity became a ceiling: impeding and curtailing movement upward. Its presumed impenetrability became justification for their delaying tactics. Even in the language of delayers—"They're keeping us down."—the effects of the ceiling are easily discernible. For advancers, adversity became a floor from which to launch upward. Its very lowness became motivation for their industry and hard-driving tactics. Their language—"We're moving on up."—amplified their perspective. This distinction between advancers and delayers, floors and ceilings is important because it explains the *cultural schizophrenia* that seems to define and plague black Americans.[2]

At one and the same time, black Americans are characterized by industry and sloth, ambition and defeat, hopefulness and helplessness. We are smart and stupid, strategic and clueless, triumphant and vanquished. Unless we recognize and relish this historic split in our purposes and deeds, we will continue to be confused regarding our identities. Even today, nearly 150 years after emancipation, we still grapple mightily with where we belong: The 'hood or beyond, struggling or beyond—black or beyond.

THEY KILLED ALL OUR LEADERS.

KEEPING IT REAL DUMB

Since the 'hood receives so much attention from the media, race profiteers, and delayers, it is here that the battle line is drawn. The battle prize is the source of identity for ourselves and our children. Fables based upon ghetto life have dominated the imagination of black people and the remainder of America. Here, it is assumed, is where *real* black persons live, where *real* black problems exist, and where our *real* psyches lie. Unfortunately, our ghetto fables have gained an enduring life of their own. We hang on reminiscently to them. Few other fables or tales have been passed on since separation from Africa. That's not our fault. It just is. Even more unfortunate is that acceptance and endorsement of ghetto fables serve greatly to maintain boundaries of what is considered black. For example, ghetto fables serve to bolster the self-esteem of underachieving black Americans while implicitly devaluing the achievements of black advancers. In common parlance, those who "keep it real"—tragically perceived as being truly and authentically black—are reinforced, while those who venture away from the rationalizations of ghetto fables are left to reinforce themselves. Not surprisingly, those who "keep it real" are also those who choose not to venture too far forward. They are, in essence, underachievers and delayers; trading high motivational levels for staying black.

 THEY PUT CRACK IN THE 'HOOD.

So what of those who achieve? Do they not have a place in black America? Are black people who grow up physically, emotionally, and psychologically outside the 'hood less black? So much of our identity has been related to adversity that those persons who achieve quite successfully have felt marginalized by black communities. They have felt outside at times, tolerated at other times, and reviled often. However, groups rarely advance as a whole. Some members will advance much more quickly than the majority, while others will advance more slowly, if at all. Such is the nature of life. My treatise is that familiarity with these ghetto fables through repeated telling from generation to generation has made them increasingly difficult to discard. We have endorsed them, unthinkingly, and they have become part of our individual and cultural identity. As such, they entrench us—physically, emotionally, and psychologically—in the 'hood. And, regarding those black persons who dare to exist physically, emotionally, and psychologically outside the 'hood, we black Americans have learned to negate, ridicule, and reject their resolve. That's right. You know it's true. Black advancers too often are criticized for pursuing the very same freedoms that our forebears only dreamed of experiencing—all in the name of community. How dare we?

ALL THEY LEFT US WAS THE 'HOOD AND CRIME.

The significance of ghetto fables in keeping us entrenched in the 'hood cannot be overstated. These fables tie us to those bygone days of seemingly interminable black struggle; days that delayers would have us believe will continue until all of us—each and every one of us—are not struggling. Tragically, we—delayers and advancers alike—stay tied to The Struggle.

Ghetto fables do not evolve. They are told again and again and again. While advancers are creating new stories and fashioning new endings to tales of adversity, delayers are ratifying old, dysfunctional outlooks and traditions. Delayers bolster each other; taking turns recounting fables. They cling to the idea that progress in the face of their pitifully predictable adversaries is unattainable. Sit in any delayer kitchen or pause on any delayer street corner and you'll hear it all day.

WE AIN'T NEVER GOT OUR FORTY ACRES AND A MULE.

..

. .

.,.

REFERENCE: (1965). Philadelphia, the corner of Germantown Avenue and Chelten Avenue

"Man, I'm trying to get it together, but the white man controls everything. Plus, we was brought over here in chains. Me and my people never had a chance."

REFERENCE: (1975). Philadelphia, same corner

"Brother, I'm trying to do right, but the white man controls everything. Plus, they done killed all our leaders. Now they telling us to pull ourselves up by the bootstraps. That's bull."

REFERENCE: (1985). Philadelphia, same corner

"Homie, I'm trying to take care of business, but the white man controls everything. We ain't never even got our forty acres and a mule. How we gonna get ahead when we can't even get the basics they owe us?"

REFERENCE: (1995). Philadelphia, same corner

"Player, we all trying to do something, but the system's against us. They put crack in the 'hood. They knew just what they was doing to destroy us. It's a cold game they playing."

REFERENCE: (2005). Philadelphia, same corner

"O.G., I'm trying to stay out of prison, but all they left us was the 'hood and crime. I gotta get paid and get mine."

Sound familiar?

Advancers, even those still stuck physically in the 'hood, are oriented toward the future. As such, they and their stories evolve. New endings are created and expected for each generation. Delayers, in contrast, maintain the same tired endings. Their existences are static. Don't believe me? Think about the last time you were back home. Did it feel as if you had entered a time warp? Same old people doing the same old stuff and telling the same old stories from fifteen, twenty-five, thirty-five years ago. Tell the truth: Did you consider, after only a few days, changing to an earlier flight on an earlier day? Or is it just me?

 # THE SYSTEM IS AGAINST US.

The continued acceptance and endorsement of black ghetto fables is justifiable only if one is invested in delaying movement forward. That is, only by holding onto old tried and true rationalizations (e.g., lack of opportunity; the evil intent of the white man), are delayers able to maintain a sense of self-efficacy. In essence, "It's not me who is responsible for my plight, it's prejudice, discrimination, racism, the legacy of slavery, ad infinitum." However, given that advancers, in the face of those same adversities, have reached and sustained monumental successes, a number of important questions beg to be answered:

How do we come to know our adversities are conquerable?
When do we realize our personal struggles are over?
How do we recognize the journey's end?
How do we perceive those of us whose struggles are already over?
When do we allow our tales of adversity to fade from delineators of identity to historical footnote?

Some of us are advancers, others delayers. Some of us are industrious, others trifling. The 'hood is temporary lodging for some of us; for others, it is permanent sanctuary. Ceilings and floors have differential significance for many of us. The recognition and embracing of these fundamental dilemmas of black identity represent crucial milestones in our individual and community development. Decreasing the omnipotence of ghetto fables is the foundation of our advancement away from The Struggle and toward black psychological freedom.

Chapter 5

WHY BIG MOMMA'S FEETS HURT SO MUCH

God could not be everywhere, so he created mothers.
—FOLK SAYING

It is beneath human dignity to lose one's individuality and become a mere cog in the machine.
—MOHANDAS K. GANDHI

In my family, Mom and Dad held dominion over us kids. If we messed up, there was no explanation to be considered, no meeting of the minds—just crushing submission. They hardly had to say a word. Just a glance from either parent was more than enough to put me firmly back in my place. Most times I wasn't even quite sure just how I had gotten out of place, but I didn't question it. I just stepped back in line. They were the law. They ruled. The only times my parents' authority could be overruled was by the High Court—the absolute potentate—the final, unchallengeable word: Big Momma.

HER MAJESTY

The influence of traditional matriarchy on black individual and community psychology has been pervasive for centuries. The role of "Big Momma" has enjoyed a special place in black community fact and lore. Divinity personified, Big Momma has been portrayed frequently through television, radio, film, and stage. Neither high nor low person, bum nor star, may challenge her domain. She is all powerful and all knowing.[1]

Ask any black person, and rather readily they'll be able to recount any number of Big Momma stories:

> I remember Big Momma in her run-over house shoes sliding 'round the house. Back sore; hips achin'; feets hurtin'. Gruntin' from the pain. You could hear her coming way before she got there. Big Momma would ease into her Easy Chair. But, 'fore too long she'd be calling you. "Baby, come on over here and helps your Big Momma out dis chair. I swear I don't know why your Mammy bought dis chair. Can't nobody never get up from here. Probably tryin' to kill me so I be out da way. But, dat's all right. I be gone soon 'nuf. Gone to Glory. Yes, Jesus!"
>
> When you really think about it, Big Momma was falling apart. But, when Big Momma told you to do something, you did it. Quick! Talking back?! You must be crazy!
>
> —Philadelphia street urchin

Funny how so physically pathetic an image could garner so much power and influence. Although Big Momma's frailties serve as counterpoint to her inner strength, her ability to nurture beyond her restricted worldview is limited. That is, while Big Momma may be a pillar of perseverance, she is at the same time a roadblock to unimagined horizons, because she can't see the full distance. Cousins, uncles, aunts, brothers, sisters, and others who may be more qualified to nurture, direct, and role model are often not accessed.

Big Momma—round, shiny, and warm—exerts a retarding effect upon development of individual freedom and healthy selves for black Americans. Her portrayal as beneficent matriarch belies her role as subjugator extraordinaire. Her dominion as final authoritative voice is both troublesome and dangerous. It disallows expressions of confidence and self-sufficiency. (Oh, no he didn't! Tell me this fool didn't say something bad 'bout Big Momma!)

Big Momma's "children" (any and all family members younger than she) are encouraged to be respectful and compliant dolts. The ubiquitous community precept that "you ain't never too grown to not listen to Big Momma" has a dampening effect upon her children's barely lit kindling of individual self-development. Big Momma's wisdom through longevity—but naiveté through lack of worldliness—compromises self-direction. Her children, protected and infantilized beyond repair, are kept from forging out. Everyone remains tethered to one of Big Momma's myriad umbilical cords. Her feets hurt so much because she has to carry so many people.

Chapter 6

SEARCHING FOR BLACK IDENTITY
Backward or Forward

Our children may learn about heroes of the past. Our task is to make ourselves architects of the future.
—Jomo Mzee Kenyatta

Ninety percent of the world's woe comes from people not knowing themselves, their abilities, their frailties, and even their real virtues. Most of us go
almost all the way through life as complete strangers to ourselves.
—Sydney J. Harris

Where do I fit in? How am I supposed to be? To whom do I look for
answers? Generation after generation, such fundamental questions of being human are faced by adolescents. The answers that they arrive at
go far in affecting their eventual self-concept and identity. Tragically, for most
black children born in the United States, race has historically commandeered
the lion's share of their answers. Its omnipresence is part of the lifeblood of our
nation. To their detriment, black adolescents have had to consider race as an
integral part of who they are.

BIRTH OF BLACK DELAYERS

Sadly, in their efforts to address questions of identity, many of today's young black persons (and I dare say a great number of their elders) find themselves possessed. Their possessor is a ghost—an apparition of things long gone. It is a poltergeist. It steers them rearward, toward the past. There they find direction for their lives; among the remnants and ashes of the civil rights era. There, they sift for answers. Rather than pursuing new, fresh ways of being human, they identify with the struggles that predominated the civil rights era. Those struggles become their struggles. From that time in history black children hear bold retorts to the questions they ask: "What does it mean to be black?" "How do I interact with people who aren't black?" "What should I expect from the world?" and "What is my place in the world?" Such questions are answered readily—although incompletely—by the political and social tenor of the 1950s and 1960s.

Failing to acknowledge the boundaries of historical context, many black children look backward to Malcolm X, Bobby Seale, Angela Davis, Martin Luther King Jr., Elijah Muhammad, Huey Newton, and a host of lesser deities for answers. For a sense of *black* identity, they orient themselves backward toward the hallowed past. Tragically, that same backward orientation inclines them to identify with yesterday's racism and oppression, while rejecting today's increased social and economic opportunities. They become delayers—girded for battle but without a clear enemy. Our children come to equate blackness with struggle. Struggle becomes central to their perception of self. In their minds one is not truly black unless struggling or downtrodden. These children forgo opportunities they perceive as antithetical to their *black* identity. They resist ideas that would bring them more in line with present context. They reject the reality of increased social and economic opportunity for black persons. Worse, they reject the role models of black persons who, by having embraced the American Dream, are not struggling or downtrodden.

Armed with only a cursory understanding of the past, they "Say It Loud," without pursuing self-sufficiency and empowerment. They shout, "I Am Somebody!" while settling to be nobodies. In exchange for clearly delineated—although constricted—identities based on the past, such persons *delay* overtures toward more expansive but undefined futures. In the end, they estrange themselves from a future they see as *white*—from the very same future that their black predecessors struggled for them to have.

Obviously these children are misguided. By and large, their role models—us—are little help in instructing them to look toward the future and away from the past. After all, Malcolm X and the others were *our* heroes, *our* role models. They were larger than life in an era that was larger than most. We lived with them and came to love them. We were touched by their magic and enthralled by their messages. And we want their messages—strong messages—to strike resonant chords in our offspring. We want their memories and dreams kept alive. After all, how could any of us bear to tell our children to look away from our heroes, our warriors in shining armor? Most of us cannot. So although the world has advanced beyond the racial issues of yesteryear, we become saddled with young warriors who desire to emulate *our* fallen, outdated heroes.

Our children must surely be misguided. Misguided by our past. Just listen to their music. Many of its messages are of hate: hatred based on race, economic class, and lifestyle—or, more succinctly, hatred of all that is perceived as *white*. In my travels, I often encounter such young persons. They are usually young pups of twenty or so years of age who are a little too well versed in the "ways of white folks." They think themselves omniscient. Surliness dominates their faces. Anger permeates their souls. As their rhetoric spews forth, I wonder how these youngsters could know so much of the 1950s and 1960s, a period well before their time. After all, young people are hardly motivated to study history. They're much too busy trying to be cool and fit in. Yet these young warriors are seemingly quite attuned to this era in American history.

The worst of these young pups adopt very extreme positions. They become caught up in rhetoric and hate. Taking the role of either archvictim or archrevolutionary, these individuals hope to rekindle an ideological fire whose embers are barely recognizable. They incorporate into their identities a hate for anything—suburbia, music, people, success—that they perceive as *white*. They reject white persons *because* they are white. According to their ravings—and sometimes lyrics—white people act conspiratorially to subjugate the bulk of black Americans.

Further, these youngsters assert that black people, as a group, will never reach equal footing with the majority of white Americans because it is "a white man's world." Some even identify with desperate philosophies of the past, suggesting that we separate ourselves from the white world—that we would do better collectively if left to ourselves, and that *our* resources, *our* schools, and *our* businesses would be best operated and patronized by and for *us*.

In searching for identity, these youngsters become swayed by the saliency of color. They come to believe that they are kindred philosophically, politically, and spiritually to those who look like them. They come to believe that there exist race-specific attitudes and behaviors. Skin color is so obvious a distinction that these youngsters, like other racists, seek to extend that distinctiveness beyond melanin to all aspects of humanness. Our children too easily accept the notion of color as purveyor of culture. This is particularly the case for children reared by unenlightened parents. These young persons are very much at risk for incorporating into their identities the saliency of color and thereby becoming snared and blinded by the past.

Obviously, an analysis of human complexities based upon race is far too simplistic. The factors that influence how humans think and act are too complex to be subsumed under the one characteristic of *race*. Individuals who are racially alike may think very differently from each other. Conversely, individuals who are racially different may think in very similar ways. For example, one might presume dissimilar goals for white liberals and black separatists. However, such persons often have similar interests regarding the progress and psyche of black people. They share an agenda that proffers up black people as perpetual victims. Both are invested in keeping us dependent or struggling or downtrodden or angry. And, as a result, we—the dependent, struggling, downtrodden, and angry—do not reach out to access the full strata of the system. We remain, in essence, fodder for their ideological fires.

You must admit that large numbers of black folk at the lower economic stratum give fuel to the fires of liberals and separatists alike. Their philosophies—liberal or separatist—have merit only as long as the flock doesn't exceed expectations. Black overachievers, for example, cannot rely strongly on either white liberal support or black separatist acceptance. Think about it.

Overachievers do not fit a prescribed way of being black. Their identities are "unknown" to us, and they are shunted by both groups for not being "black enough."

The power of race in affecting how young black persons see themselves and others is a very important consideration in the movement toward psychological freedom. Race delivers a regulator of sorts to the development, range, and expression of one's being. Its specter often serves to suppress free and unencumbered enunciation of who you are. From my own childhood three different persons significantly affected my racial identity, and thereby my psychological freedom.

Diane

Diane, a white liberal person, befriended my mother some years ago. When I was very young, Diane was genuinely and sincerely concerned with our family. She was there to help us with loans and emotional support. She sort of adopted us, and she always came through whenever times were tough. But things became different as our family became increasingly self-sufficient. Somewhat predictably, Diane changed. It seemed her friendship and loyalty were based in large part upon a relationship in which she would always have the upper hand. As long as we were her "project," she was happy. Long-term dependency was her aim. That is, her liberalism went only so far as to help us out of a current problem. Once my mother's favorite son became increasingly more educated and self-reliant, Diane's relationship with us changed. It was ever so slight at first, but as I became more degreed and achieved beyond her wildest dreams, things changed. Diane's relationship with Mom became somewhat strained. I believe the source of that strain was independence. Once we were perceived as independent, the niceties ceased.

This taught me that once you draw equal to your benefactors, things can become a bit funky. For Diane, anything short of equality was acceptable. She seemed to be saying to us, through her white liberalism, "We want y'all to do well, but not *that* damned well!"

Barbara

Barbara, a black grassroots activist, always pushed the neighborhood children to achieve. "Challenge the white man and become successful," she would state vigorously. However, Barbara had her own way of impeding the progress of others. As long as black persons aspired to become teachers, athletes, preachers, or entertainers, her world was right. Their achievements coincided with her game plan for us all. In her eyes, these professions—noble as they are—fell within an acceptable range of achievement for black persons. She believed that attainment below that range meant the underachiever's efforts had been compromised by the white man. Anything attained above that range meant the overachiever had sold out to—that's right!—that very same white man. Obviously, the white man figured heavily in her worldview.

When I and others began to exceed the expectations of even the most optimistic of neighborhood folk, Barbara became uncomfortable. It seemed that as long as she perceived some incongruity between the achievements of white folks and black folks, "her game had no shame." That is, she could run her rhetoric past benefactors in order to fund, financially and morally, her philosophies. But when faced with black overachievers, she withdrew her support. Barbara began to attend less to those of us who had understood, accepted, and mastered the formulae for success. Given her investment in uplifting en masse her people, Barbara's inattention to budding advancers was to be expected. After all, advancers do not need or are unwilling to await the uplifting. An opportunity—fair, or sometimes less than fair—is their only requirement.

However, unexpectedly, Barbara came to view us as threats of sorts. I believe, in her eyes, we became apart from the community, apart from "the people." We had ascended too quickly and too independently. It wasn't that Barbara wasn't happy for us or proud of us. It was that we were now foreign to her. And our foreign success, but familiar skin color, drew steam away from her uplifting the community en masse philosophy. Just think of the ramifications if a successful kid or two became twenty or forty kids?

Barbara knew that if black kids continued to achieve on their own—without guilt, intimidation, or rhetoric—eventually one of her benefactors would ask, "If *those* kids can do it without our help, why can't others?" and "Why do we need you and your programs?" Overachievement was antithetical to her game plan. Its recognition could bankrupt her entire approach. It was as if Barbara was saying, through her black grassroots activism, "We want y'all to do well, but not *that* damned well!"

Harry

Harry (who would later change his name to something more relevant for the 1960s) moved into the neighborhood during my fourteenth year of life. In my opinion, Harry was one of the original black militants. He talked of black nationalism, pan-Africanism, economic isolationism, and mistrust of all white persons long before most militant groups reached their height in popularity. I remember him as the first person I knew who used the terms *Brother* and *Sister*. He sported black leather jackets, black turtlenecks, and a manner of uncompromising surliness. For the times, he was blackness personified.

Except for an occasional forage to the ice cream man, Harry would while away his time in Vernon Park. There, among the remnants of its rare gardens and the previous night's drug abuse, he would remain, available to anyone who was interested in hearing "the truth." Predictably, his truth included the evilness of the white race.

"It's a natural consequence of their very nature," Harry would preach.

Just look at their history. Everywhere they've been there's been destruction, slavery, oppression, and poverty. They always say it's us that look like apes and monkeys? But it's a fact that if you shave a gorilla, underneath he's white. That's right. Bet you didn't know that, did you? They say we're primitive? Well, our ancestors were royalty and studied in universities while theirs were living in caves afraid of fire. We have to separate ourselves from them. Not be soiled by their demon ways. We need to create a separate nation, build our own communities and businesses, and leave them to their evil. Otherwise, we will continue to be poisoned by their scandalous ways.

Six days a week Harry would offer his view of the world—sometimes commanding large audiences, sometimes only an inebriate or two. Prominent in his speeches were references to those persons he held in equal disdain with the evil whites: the Uncle Toms, the sellouts, the step-and-fetch-its, and the bootlickers of the black community.

"Those damned Uncle Tom Negroes," he would snarl. "They're the worst. They're so busy kissing up to the white man and trying to be white, they don't even know what's happening and how they've been tricked."

People like Harry always amazed me. While critical of their achieving brethren, they rarely offered any substantive or viable alternative, only rhetoric and derision. Any black person who adopted the American Dream was rejected by Harry as selling out, as compromising his *black* identity. Black advancers represented a serious threat to Harry and those of his ilk. Their success in "the white world" compromised Harry's ability to generalize evil intent to all white persons. These black people were, to Harry's chagrin, doing too well. He seemed to be saying, through his black separatism, "We want y'all to do well, but not *that* damned well!"

Folks like Diane, Barbara, and Harry influence children and how they see themselves. Irrespective of gender, ethnicity, or even politics, such role models present attitudes and behaviors that endorse the ill-conceived dichotomy of *us* and *them*. They assert that "those people" believe and behave in ways that are different than our own. They shout, "We are *us* and they are *them*." Then they go about blithely perpetuating their false dichotomy. Worse, their examples encourage black children to voice the same racism and separatism that many of us have fought to eradicate. Parenthetically, it is a racism and separation that exceedingly few of these children have known *except* through our examples.

Children are not born with racist and separatist ideas. They learn them, from role models steeped in past separatism and past racism. Accordingly, children do not live in a world characterized by the same racism and separatism of our past. No longer are differences between people highlighted in children's minds and reinforced through state and federal law. Children, black or otherwise, exist in a world that is *not* the same as a generation or two ago. Of course, strongholds of racism and separatism still exist. But I believe these strongholds are exceedingly few in reality, and predominate only in our retroactive minds.

VEERING OFF THE ROAD TO FREEDOM

Overtures toward nonacceptance of others and separatism actually fly in the face of the very civil rights activists our young people seek to emulate. Many persons—some famous, but most anonymous—have protested, fought, been jailed, and died in an effort to have black people woven into the American fabric, not as a monolith of blackness or as separate tenants on American soil, but as fully participating and benefiting American citizens. Yet these youngsters are eager to cast us adrift. Apparently simplistic dichotomies like *black* and *white* or *them* and *us* are attractive to the young and the naive. They explain the world in simple terms that are easily understood. The subtle shades of gray that capture real life are avoided because they take real effort to work through.

I sense much fear and apprehension in the protests of the youngsters and their mentors. Fear of becoming lost in a sea of self-determination. Fear that content rather than color will become a reality and the rule in social discourse. Fear that if such were the case, they would be found wanting—having to rely on attributes and achievements defined by the past. One must take responsibility for oneself and not blame others for one's own failings. Separatism and nonacceptance of others must certainly be the final and desperate gasps of the young and the naive at maintaining a sense of *black* identity and shared oppression. After all, would mature and intelligent persons really want to remain separate? Would they really want their individualities and idiosyncrasies leveled by skin color? It seems that we've already had those experiences in America. It sounds like fear of the future to me.

Our blackness, *my* blackness, *their* blackness, and *your* blackness trap us by color. Be black, think black, buy black, and stay black—all of these trap us in thought and deed. We are relegated to a box labeled "black." We become and

are forced to be colors—not humans with individual souls but objects constricted by the overinclusiveness of color. We are *black* women, *black* men,
black children—and are correspondingly restricted by this qualifier. We are
restricted. This must surely be the case because one can't possibly entertain
one's humanness if one is first concerned with and objectified by one's blackness. Moreover, in our social interactions, we become hesitant to reveal or dis-
close to others—black or otherwise—our humanness. How can we ever be free
in thought and deed if we must first and foremost be black? Can we permit
ourselves and each other such freedom? Will others allow us such freedom?

I personally hold little hope for people. My suspicion is that humans will
never be able to advance to a stage where external characteristics become
inconsequential. As a species, we are much too primitive to overcome color,
ethnicity, and gender as assumed delineators of behavior. Our primitive nature
is aptly demonstrated through our anthropology. After two hundred thousand
years of development, biological and social evolution, and "civilization," we
humans still resolve many of our conflicts the same old way—we kill.

I often imagine there are beings from other worlds and galaxies looking
upon us with wary eyes. I think of an alien mom (like any good mommy)
saying to her offspring, "Yes, you can go out to play, Junior. But, stay out of
danger. And remember what I told you: 'Don't go anywhere near Earth!'"

TOWARD BEING HUMAN

How can we begin to help our young people with their questions of identity if
we ourselves continue to look backward, fearful that our blackness will no
longer be a mitigator of circumstances for us, that we might actually be held
accountable for our outcomes? For many of us, to be judged on the merits of
our skills, personalities, and motivations runs counter to a position and status
that we have, in our minds, *earned*. It is the position of top victim—a highly
valued and reserved place in the American psyche. This is a place where self-
defeat, personal foibles, and inadequacies are rarely questioned—a place where
membership provides, at least psychologically, a protected status.

I would hope that all sensible persons would rail against those who would throw us backward into the shadows, fearful of self-responsibility, self-determination, progress, and harmony. As America becomes increasingly less color conscious, black Americans become put upon to choose. The choice is one of inclusion or exclusion. The choice is to embrace the future with all its benefits *and* challenges, or to clutch desperately to the restrictive and stagnant familiarities of the past.

Those persons who preach separatism, nonacceptance of others, and a tragically constricted *black* identity claim their philosophies are most closely aligned with the past struggles of our revered heroes. By association, they consider themselves somehow nobler than those of us foolish enough to toil in the present with an eye toward the future. Sentinels to the past such as Minister Louis Farrakhan, Rev. Al Sharpton, and Rev. Jesse Jackson claim it is *they* who are keeping alive the spirits of Malcolm, Martin, Harriet, and others. How truly wrong are these black men and women. The message of our martyred benefactors is not one of exclusion and identification with the past. Collectively, they enjoined us to be included in the American family, not as distant relations but as central and contributing relatives. Our legacy is only *defined* by the past. Its attainment and realization lies in the future.

We *must* embrace the future and inclusion. The actions we take will be crucially important for still-to-be-born-black children, who will, in their time, search for their own identities. Unless we are able to let go of the past, future generations will be as unprepared for their world as are today's young pups. If our youth are left unadvised, they will likely incorporate into their identities the false and contrived anger of their assumed vanguard—the worst among the rap and hip-hop musicians. They will believe the messages of hate emanating from these entertainers are real, that these entertainers are the vanguard for a people disaffected by their status in American society. But they are not a vanguard. They are entertainers. They entertain, but, more importantly, they sell false pride and false hate. Not unlike large corporations that feed off poor black kids, these entertainers join the frenzy, gobbling up money and futures. Naively, our children—and a great number of their elders—believe that because the shark is black it won't bite.

The presumptions of race that have dominated our society for the last four centuries are being rejected. Today, we are experiencing a revolution. Its nonviolence belies its omnipresence. It is not a revolution of weapons and rhetoric, but of inclusion and pluralism. We are indeed benefiting from the efforts of our forebears. We have become integral parts of the American society and culture. No longer can whiteness or blackness of skin be used exclusively to define quality of character.

The goal of the twenty-first century is to help all people—including blacks—learn not to employ color as a qualifier for opportunities, affiliations, and respect. Rather, the content of an individual's character should be foremost. It means truly processing the ideas of the relatedness of all humans, and judging each other not by color, but by character. These ideas help define the foundation for positive relations among racial and ethnic groups. More importantly, they provide a groundwork for the exploration of identity for adolescents facing a less color-conscious society.

Chapter 7

THE BLUE AND THE RED
Just Hangin' 'round the 'Hood

We cannot be satisfied as long as the Negro's basic mobility is from a smaller ghetto to a larger one.
—MARTIN LUTHER KING JR.

[The ghetto is] a kind of concentration camp, and not so many people survive it.
—JAMES BALDWIN

Many of our neighborhoods are dangerous places. Chicago's South Side, North Philly, Miami's Liberty City, and the Hill District in Pittsburgh are among hundreds of places where one's life can be wantonly and capriciously extinguished. Every single day in such places, someone is hurt or killed by criminal gangs, by police abuses, or just by the bullshit that generally befalls ghetto inhabitants. The daily business of negotiating one's way through drive-by shootings, stupid neighborhood feuds, and random violence is often near impossible. Walk-ups, stabbings in barrooms, and questionable police encounters threaten physical integrity. Guilty and innocent alike are subjected to a daily regimen of physical danger. However, physical danger presents itself as just one of many significant threats to residents.

91

Scene: ON THE AVENUE

Sister #1: Y'all hear 'bout G-Man? How he got beat down then shot up?

Brother #1: Yeah, I just did hear. Them's the breaks. He should have known what was up.

Sister #2: Obviously the boy wasn't hip to what was crackin'.

Brother #2: These streets are dangerous. You gotta take care of yourself.

Sister #3: Shouldn't had his ass out here if he couldn't hang.

Brother #3: I can't believe he ain't have nobody watchin' his back.

ASSAULT AND BATTERY TO THE MIND

Persons who live in dangerous places are victimized daily by an onslaught to the psyche, besieged mentally by the mayhem of ghetto existence. These threats to psychological health, although more difficult to discern, are arguably more hazardous and abundant than physical threats. Poor support for efforts to escape, daily instruction in the use of rationalization and delay to protect fragile egos, pervasive models of self-defeat, and poor parenting are omnipresent in such neighborhoods. In such places there also exist pervasive attitudes that not only accept but aggrandize violence, danger, and death. Violence and death are often perceived as unavoidable facts of neighborhood life. Residents commonly believe that all who live in the 'hood should be acclimated to the presence of violence and death. They believe that for the initiated, signs of imminent danger abound. At street corner postmortems you can hear survivors of the most recent urban outrage repeat the ghetto dwellers' axiom: "Don't have your ass out here if you can't hang!"

Scene: MY 'HOOD, YOUR 'HOOD, THEIR 'HOOD

Survivor #1: Man, that was real funky how that kid got hemmed up between them gangs.
Survivor #2: Little G dead over nothing.
Survivor #1: Them kids gotta learn to keep low.
Survivor #2: You ain't lying! I learned that when I was *real* young.
Survivor #1 (while offering a high-five): Who you tellin'? Me too!

Such attitudes (and the morally bankrupt persons who proffer them) do much to tax the minds of those persons battling to survive the 'hood. Because, acclimated or not, violence, mayhem, and death are too often unpredictable in such places. It rarely matters whether somebody has your back or you know what's up. Children and adults die without warning. That's why I don't hang out in the 'hood. It's a dangerous place. However, if a person has no choice but to be there, then there is much to be said for spending as much time as possible inside one's home—relatively safe from those persons outside who act as animals.

As a child, to escape the carnage I went to school, to the library, to any-place where I was shielded from those who would threaten me physically and psychologically. Like a slave escaping bondage, I sought to break free of my physical and mental captors. I'd sneak and slither through my neighborhood as if aboard a latter-day Underground Railroad: heart racing, palms sweating, peeking around corners, listening for the voices of my captors, barely ahead of the barking hounds. Fearful of my pursuers, I'd work my way to my safe houses: libraries, schools, museums. Once there, I'd relieve my mental burden with reading or conversation with others trying to escape. Afterward, I'd sneak back home and hope for another day. I didn't hang out on the streets. A person could get killed there. One of my more poignant memories of growing up was my fourteenth birthday. Sitting in my mother's kitchen, I reflected, "Wow, I made it to fourteen! Wonder if I'll make it to fifteen?" I repeated this operatic scene for four terror-filled years! You see, I had reached prime gang war victim/police brutality statistic/killed over some bullshit age. And with the passing of each successive year, until I escaped to college, I felt as if I was living on borrowed time.

Persons who hung out on the streets or went to house parties were, in my opinion, just plain crazy. I suppose my self-imposed imprisonment was also crazy. But, given my surroundings, one could hardly argue with my prudence. A constricted social circle simply increased my life expectancy. It seemed a kid was killed every week hanging out on the streets or at a house party. Who in their right mind would be crazy enough to venture into that fray? Certainly not me.

HELPING OUR CHILDREN SURVIVE

Another of my important memories of the 'hood came after I had successfully escaped to college. I had not visited home for quite a long time. Late in my senior year, I discovered that three of my Philadelphia brethren also had not ventured home in their senior year. Fascinatingly, we all shared the same fear, as expressed by one pal: "After all I went through to get this far, I'll be damned if I'm gonna get shot or stabbed now over some bullshit and never graduate. I'm graduating first and then taking my chances." What a hero's welcome to return to!

Persons who at present have no choice but to live in the 'hood must learn to negotiate both its physical *and* its psychological threats. Each neighborhood presents different challenges. Residents must therefore determine which negotiation strategies are functional for their particular surroundings. In some cases, individuals might have to band with others for mutual physical and psychological protection. Others might have to wind their way through dangerous streets and even more dangerous role models. Because awaiting our children—just down the street or around the corner—are chronic rationalizations, destruction, and role models of self-defeat.

Scene:
JUST DOWN THE STREET AND AROUND THE CORNER

Robert: I can't wait 'til I graduate. As soon as I can I'm moving over to the North Side, away from all this craziness.
Goldie: You want to move out?! Robert, you trippin.' You ain't no better than nobody else. You black and yo' ass is always gonna be black. Don't be trying to front.
Robert: I just thought it would be nice to have a safe place to crib.
Goldie: Boy, going to college done got you all messed up. You been around them too much. Keep it real, brother! Keep it real!

Parenting

The attitudes that parents exhibit can serve to bolster or hamper young minds as they search for the "right" roads to travel. Mature and responsible parents can help their children feel safe and supported by encouraging them in their endeavors. Small actions such as walking them to the library or helping them to study go far in bolstering the resolve of children as they resist the animals of the community. Parents: if you can, move out. Do not accept the idea that only "the uppity" want to move out. It is more likely that only the uppity and the weak-willed want you to stay.

Unfortunately, far too many children are saddled with parents who are not mature or responsible enough to support their efforts. Support and guidance are likely difficult to muster for parents who birthed their children during adolescence. A twenty-six-year-old with an eleven- or twelve-year-old child may view that child as more of a burden or trophy than as a young person in need of parenting. These parents are likely still addressing their own issues of adolescence. Such junior parents are themselves still very much in need of guidance. At times, their immaturity will preempt their ability to look beyond themselves. As a result, cultivation of their offspring's potentiality will suffer at the hands of parents who perceive their children's dreams as capricious, expensive, or psychologically threatening.

Feelings of resentment and jealousy may arise when these junior parents are faced with a child who, perhaps too easily, exceeds their own achievements. It is not unusual for such parents to lash out at their young charges, whom they perceive as threats. And, thus, a child with potential may well have that potentiality crushed by a parent pressed to maintain his or her own tenuous sense of superiority. Through intimidation, lack of emotional support, and ridicule parents may devastate an offspring psychologically. 'Round the 'hood some threats are as close as home.

Parents' support groups can be particularly valuable in helping young parents address their own unmet psychological needs. Whether led by a professional therapist or not, such groups often provide insights to everyday living and a future beyond next week. Even if such groups only meet for one hour each month, they can work to bring perspective to a seemingly mundane and routine life, as well as provide an arena through which frustrations may be voiced. For example, a parent who is trying to maintain a job (or two) while trying to keep a child motivated and safe can feel quite overwhelmed. Emotional support can be crucial in fostering motivated and successful families. Contrary to popular black thought, going to see a therapist doesn't mean you're crazy.

Reading, 'Riting, 'Rithmetic

Whether in elementary school or college, children need to feel supported in their endeavors. Since the overwhelming majority of us are not athletically or artistically gifted, education is the most accessible door out of the 'hood. Everyone knows how important education is to success. Even bums on the street enjoin kids to get an education. Still, even in the face of such consensus, so many parents are woefully unaware of their children's academic potential.

Yet many of these same parents complain, day in and day out, about schools not doing their jobs. Such complaints have always been interesting to me. How can anyone legitimately chastise an educational system who is not intimately involved in her children's education? Schools and teachers can be helpful in attaining goals, but they are not guarantors of dreams.

In tough neighborhoods, school is often a place where education happens secondarily. Problems with discipline, violence, drug cultures, and extortion compromise effective lesson plans. These are our schools, in our neighborhoods, teaching our children. Yet we permit thugs to control them. Our children might as well be educated on the streets. And, no doubt, many are. Thinking black, being black, and staying black—to the delight of black delayers and race profiteers—are the lesson plans of the streets.

Education is a passport to success in this country. It will take you on journeys only whispered and dreamed about by little ghetto dwellers. But in order to take the journey, one must carry the passport. Without it, children can only complain and blame others—as their parents do—while they miss out on their journeys. The light in which education is cast by parents has a significant effect upon children's valuation of it. If parents value education, so will their children.

Examples abound of parental noninvolvement in their children's education. Look around any ghetto street—day or night. Too often school attendance is viewed only as compulsory—something mandated by the state. For others, school is a babysitter, providing five to six hours of relief—Monday through Friday—from the obligations of parenthood.

It is somewhat understandable that parents would want their children out of the house. After caring for them constantly for three to five years, any sane person would relish a break. However, we need to earnestly take an extremely active role in the education of our children. After all, they are *our* children. They don't belong to teachers, principals, or superintendents—they belong to us. We must attend to their needs. Black children can ill afford inattention.

Despite the desires of lazy-assed parents, schools are not factories charged with fashioning viable products. Too many parents behave as if their children were automobiles to be sent to the shop. They plead, "Here is my child. Take this person for twelve years. Tinker, tune, and lubricate, and give back to me a

Scene: 7:15 AM, MONDAY MORNING
AT THE JOHNSON RESIDENCE

Ms. Johnson (yelling up the stairs): Darnell! Darnell! Get up, boy!
You gonna be late again.
[Fifteen minutes later]
Ms. Johnson (standing near her sleeping son): Darnell! Boy, I'm
tired fightin' you every damned mornin' 'bout school.
Darnell: I don't know why I got to keep going there no way. We
ain't learnin' nothin', and I could get stabbed or shot in them
hallways.
Ms. Johnson: So you just want to lay there. Boy, you just like
your father. And you gonna be a dummy just like him if you
don't go to school.
Darnell: Aw, Mom.
Ms. Johnson: Look, boy. I'm done with it. I don't care where
your ass goes, but you leavin' here!

well-mannered, motivated, and educated person." But it is we who are responsible for the education of our children, no one else. They are ours. In this country every child is owed educational opportunities. But opportunities have to be approached and utilized. Otherwise, they are just opportunities—dormant and unrealized. Don't let thugs, children acting like fools, irresponsible parents, delayers, educators, race profiteers, or even *you* kill your child's opportunities. Take your responsibilities to heart.

Parents should also hold school administrators and teachers responsible for their share. Years of battling children, budget cuts, and lack of support may incline teachers and administrators toward indifference, but they are nonetheless responsible for their share in this community endeavor. In many cases, it will be important to communicate your involvement in your child's education directly to her or his teacher. Although other kids might be acting like fools—as are their parents—teachers must know that *your* child and *your* family values education. They must contribute their share. But you can't forget your share. Begin by informing teachers that rearing advancers, not delayers, is your family's goal.

The World Beyond the 'Hood

When I work with parents, there are a number of questions I invariably pose.

Question #1: How much are you responsible for your child's education and how much is the school responsible?

Usually, estimates hover around 20 to 30 percent parent and 70 to 80 percent school. When one considers that many schools are little more than child warehouses on 8:00 AM to 3:00 PM shifts, these estimates represent grave perspectives for our communities. Many schools are ill equipped to handle the many problems facing today's children. Threats of death, teen pregnancy, and the acceptance of rationalizations are set to thwart your child's potential. And even if your child is enrolled in a school that is performing a relatively good job, much of education happens outside of classrooms. Exploration of the environment and the mind, imaginative activities, science and art museum trips, interaction with the diversity of cultures and people in our cities, and family viewing of educational programs are just a few of the learning vehicles in which parents may participate.

Question #2: Are there books in your home?

Amazingly, very few complaining parents have books of any substance in their homes. Save *TV Guide*, *Ebony*, *Essence*, and a Bible, many homes are devoid of literature. Moreover, children never see their parents—by far their most influential role models—reading books. Instead, the great opiate—television—serves as the purveyor of culture and knowledge. I am unsure of the original source, but some individual once said, "If you want information kept from black people, then put it in a book." Disturbingly, for some, there is much more than a kernel of truth to this observation.

Books are the only miracles of humans. Their transcendental and enriching powers are immense. Books can mercifully serve as escapes from physically, emotionally, and psychologically debilitating conditions. As a child, the books I read by US, Russian, French, and other authors helped me to consider and envision worlds that were not immediate and were barely imaginable to me. They took me away from the constrictions of my immediate world and delivered me—if only temporarily—to the unlimited expanse of my adopted world. Most important, they girded me for one more day among the monsters. It is hardly enough to instruct your child to read books while you change channels. You must demonstrate the importance of reading.

> Children have never been very good listeners to their elders, but have never failed to imitate them.
> —James Baldwin

Question #3: When was the last time you let your child express herself to you?

Parents are often so tired from trying themselves to survive—physically, emotionally, and psychologically—that the last thing they want to hear is a child's opinion. Too often, children are shut down emotionally and psychologically by parents who, after hours of feeling ineffectual at work, are inclined to make damned sure that they are in control at home. Words like "If I want your opinion, then I'll give it to you." "Be quiet! Grown folks are talking." "You ain't grown." "I brought you into this world, and I'll take your little ass out." do little to help young minds grow and prosper. Rather, such words stifle creativity, confidence, motivation, and self-worth. The child grows to be uncertain, intimidated, reluctant, and with little self-worth—but he is obedient.

By stressing and demonstrating the importance of books, school, and life beyond the 'hood, parents teach children that more is available to them than is present in their immediate physical and psychological environment. This is crucially important for a child endeavoring to expand and move beyond what is in front of her. Physically, emotionally, and psychologically, 'hoods can be extremely dangerous places to exist. But they are not unconquerable. Education and parental involvement are invaluable pieces in helping children survive the onslaughts. While trying to survive, people should endeavor to do all that is possible to get out. The general mentality in such places is conducive not to success, but to continued struggle, the thwarting of dreams, and the courting of failure.

ESCAPING THE 'HOOD

For what earthly reason do people stay in the 'hood? The 'hood is the mother lode for race profiteers. Their fortunes await them there. If you live there you are gold for them—pitifully treated consumers buying their products and philosophies while funding their lives in politics and business. The 'hood is their stronghold, the place where seldom they are questioned about the utility of their philosophies or the real benefits of their products. People who reside in the 'hood are an inexhaustible supply of consumers of the bunk of race profiteers. You are a captive audience, chained by your own history and cultural inertia.

There is little that is redeeming about the 'hood. I can think of no reason—not one—that would justify remaining there. It is an unlikely place to foster strength of character and knowledge of self. Lifelong lessons and models of responsible behavior are not the best there. Nor are the odds of living a long life. Why do you stay—particularly if you have children?

Oh, I can hear the apologists now. How insensitive that Dr. Davison is. How unfeeling. Doesn't he realize that some people have no choice but to live there? Doesn't he know that years of—Readers, recognize where you are now: Here's where the nonsense starts—prejudice, discrimination, and racism have caused blah, blah, blah, blah, blah? Forget what apologists and race profiteers are hawking. Bottom line is this: The 'hood is supposed to be temporary lodging in your family's journey to independence, self-sufficiency, and freedom. It was never supposed to be the last stop of the advancement locomotive. Not one of our forebears ever conceived it as such. So please spare me and other advancers the rhetoric. Obviously many residents of the 'hood have forgotten its function as launching pad. In too many paralyzed minds and in too many hearts misaligned with the past, the 'hood has evolved from launching pad to last desperate bastion for "real" black Americans.

Perhaps if residents of the 'hood remained silent while doing little or nothing to advance, then the increasing negative attention from critics could be avoided. But many residents do not remain silent. While neglecting their own family's progression, these people audaciously challenge those of us who have not been neglectful. Loudly they cry, "Give back to the community!" Thunderously they demand, "Don't forget where you come from!" Under the threat of rescinding our black membership status, they collectively enjoin us to not forget "the brothers and sisters" still in the 'hood. What utter nonsense. I take this stand here and now: The 'hood is not where you want to be. If violence, death, drugs, inertia, crime, and incarceration exist where you live, then where you live is not where you want to be. So please don't expend your energy fixing up the 'hood. Don't patronize the corner mom-and-pop stores. Don't try to better the schools. All this contradicts the real issue and diverts where your energy should be spent. That is, you and yours are supposed to be trying to get *out* of the 'hood, not stay and make it prettier and more viable.

I think we have lost sight of where we are supposed to be going. We have lost sight of what our grandparents and great-grandparents wanted for us when they relocated north during the Great Migration. *Move out* as soon as is humanly possible! If you are unwilling to move for your own sake, then move for the sakes of your forebears and your offspring. Remember that you are the present traveler in a series of steps marking your family's progression. You are a sojourner in a series of temporary settings, from slavery to sharecropping to family farm to migration to the north to the 'hood. Is the 'hood your family's final stop? Aren't there more steps? Shouldn't there be more steps? Why have you stopped stepping? Being urgent about leaving the 'hood has nothing to do with being ashamed of being black. Residents, fueled by race profiteers, act like there's something nobler or more genuine or more *real* about black people who live in the 'hood. Nonsense! To the contrary, moving beyond the 'hood has everything to do with being black and being prideful and continuing your family's intergenerational progression. *That's* real!

If I could save only ten dollars a week for two years to come up with a thousand dollars for a deposit on another apartment in a decent, integrated, and upwardly mobile neighborhood, then I would do just that. I'd take all my pennies and I would *move out*. If I had to work extra hours or an extra job for a year or so in order to save the money, then I would do that and *move out*. If I had to find a partner or a mate or a friend who was similarly minded and together with that person start saving enough to move out, then I would do that and *move out*. I'd look for a place where I could rear my children and exist without hazards, but with calm and peace in my life.

There is nothing magical about the 'hood and nothing special about being able to live there. Surviving its dangers does not make you more real. It does not make you a better or stronger person, but, sadly, one who is compromised and restricted in your psychological growth, world perspective, and interactions with others. Is black heritage there in the 'hood? Yes, maybe part of it. But your future and legacy lie elsewhere. They lie where your forebears envisioned: beyond the 'hood.

> In the ghettos the white man has built for us, he has forced us not to aspire to greater things, but to view life as survival.
> —MALCOLM X

Chapter 8

SINGING THE BLUES

If you think poor, you are poor.
 —WALLY AMOS

Man is sometimes extraordinarily, passionately, in love with suffering.
 —FYODOR MIKHAILOVICH DOSTOEVSKY

Why do some people, generation after generation, remain poor? They're poor. Their mommas and their daddies are poor. And now it seems their children are hurtling headlong toward poverty—hurtling with frightening deliberateness and haste.

For years, humans have searched for explanations of poverty's resistance to eradication. Researchers have conducted hundreds of studies in an attempt to understand the mechanics that maintain and perpetuate impoverished conditions. Social activists have worked endlessly, hoping their service would somehow lessen poverty's debilitating effects on individuals and families. Government programs have offered training, employment, and millions of dollars to fight the perpetuity of poor conditions. Yet, despite these efforts as well as the availability of endless opportunities in the United States, poverty remains virulent. Statistics compiled through our most recent census suggest that one

Scene: 1970. PHILADELPHIA—CORNER OF
GERMANTOWN AVENUE AND PRICE STREET

Sonny: Little nappy head boy! Where you going with them books?
JD: To school.
Sonny: To school, huh? Well then you must have some lunch
    money. Right?
JD: Well, no. Not really.
Sonny: You lying. Let me have a quarter!

[1995—Same corner]
Sonny: Hey, JD! Man, where you been? I ain't seen you in a long
    time.
JD: I been away.
Sonny: Prison?
JD: No. School, traveling, raising my boys.
Sonny: Like that? Man, that's cool. I wanted to go to college
    and travel like you. I ain't never seen nothing past Jersey.
    Man! That crack done messed us up. The government's
    scandalous putting that stuff on the streets. A whole bunch
    of brothers is on that stuff. Ain't no way for none of us to get
    ahead. Education system don't let no brothers come up.
    Nothing but jail and the streets. It's just all messed up. My
    first is upstate and my youngest is out here somewhere.
[Sonny pauses for a few reflective moments.]
Sonny: Hey man, can you let me hold a few dollars?

out of every six American families lives in poverty. Moreover, 11 percent of
children born in the United States are born into poverty. These numbers
remain essentially unchanged from the previous US Census in 1990.

Research and social service efforts notwithstanding, it seems an understanding and delineation of the causes of poverty—no matter how exhaus-

Consider Cecil: a young man of twenty-five years of age who believes the system holds no place for him except at bottom. His sense of self and outlook toward life are greatly affected.

Cecil: Man, ain't no jobs out there for a brother. Real black men—brothers like me—ain't got no chance out there.

Voice of Reason: Actually Cecil, there *are* jobs out there for you. They might not start at fifty thousand a year, but they're out there.

Cecil: Yeah, maybe if I had gone to Harvard or something. But my people didn't have no Harvard money.

Voice of Reason: Actually Cecil, you don't have to have a Harvard education. Most jobs only want you to be qualified and motivated. They want you to apply yourself and be presentable. You just saggin' and laggin'.

Cecil: It's because I'm black. If I was white we wouldn't even be having this conversation. I could get all the education in the world. Education don't change what people see first, and that's skin color.

tive—does little to help those affected to move beyond its effects. Enumerating of the causes of poverty—along with plausible excuses for people's poor efforts to escape—may actually be injurious psychologically to people's motivation to escape its hold. For some individuals, the causes are rather quickly employed as rationalizations for their inability to escape their circumstances.

People can be quite artful in their efforts to present themselves as blameless. And, as with other of society's "victims," rationalization can be used to protect self-esteem—even that of the impoverished. Whenever people are faced with their ineffectuality, self-delusion may be much more palatable a dish than self-examination.

Psychologically, poverty is associated with rescue. And much too often, the rescuer is perceived as someone other than oneself. White people, the government, the system, even upwardly mobile black persons have variously been charged with taking care of the less fortunate. However, when one accepts the notion that rescue comes from outside oneself, an inertia is created, an inertia that fosters waiting. Waiting for racism to end. Waiting for Judgment Day. Waiting for reparations. Waiting on that settlement. Waiting for that lottery number to hit.

In so many forms, the impoverished await rescue or, at minimum, reparations for past injustices they feel precipitated their present circumstances. That the system owes to each of its citizens a decent living is a point of much debate. But irrespective of whether you believe this claim, there remains one undeniable and harsh reality: Poverty has been part of human history for centuries. It has been here and will continue to be here. The issue is not whether the system should eradicate poverty. Nor is the issue whether individuals should be responsible for their own livelihood. Rather, the issue is whether one chooses to wait for the outcome of these debates. One must choose whether to wait for rescue or to save oneself. One must decide whether to orchestrate with all one's might a successful future, or to sing the blues:

𝄞 DA DA DA DA DA
I was born and raised in the lap of poverty,
DA DA DA DA DA
Knew 'bout dealers and hypes before I was three.
DA DA DA DA DA
Each day you know I do all that I can,
DA DA DA DA DA
But I can't get nowhere 'cause of that damned white man.

Unlike most tunes, the blues transcends generations. Its tones lament the wrongfulness of present conditions. Its beat measures the lamenter's worldview. Parents teach it to their children, who teach it to their own. One would think that after hearing the blues lamented repeatedly, listeners would be motivated to change its messages for themselves, or, mercifully, for their children—that they would heed its messages and attempt to change their lives. But this seems to be the case with too few listeners. Most do not vary from the rhythm. Most are much too busy keeping sway to the beat. The latest rationalizations compromise their motivation. Not until these listeners reach thirty years of age or so do they actually begin to reflect on their lives and hear the message of the lyrics. For many, by the time they recognize the futility of singing the blues, it is too late. They find themselves anchored by children, abusive and nonsupportive spouses, drugs, motivational lethargy, poor choices, and chronic rationalizations. It's now too difficult and embarrassing to recapture their wasted youth. There are just too many hassles to obtain more education or training. So they dismiss those pestering, intrusive thoughts that admonish them for their lack of foresight. They look to the rhetoric and begin to sing:

    🎼 DA DA DA DA DA
My baby needs shoes; I ain't got a dime,
DA DA DA DA DA
Can't find me no job 'cause I just done time.
DA DA DA DA DA
I said, "Brother dear, Can I use your gun?"
DA DA DA DA DA
'Cause tonight I might have to rob me someone.

It is unfortunate that people take so many years to realize the futility of singing the blues. During my adolescence and young adulthood, I watched as my peers laid the groundwork for their later singing of the blues. Being cool and being homeboys set them up. Talking almost exclusively about drugs, gangs, sex, parties, and hanging out destined them for later singing of the blues. I was never one to believe that everyone needed to prepare to become psychologists, surgeons, or lawyers; it just seemed important that everyone try to achieve beyond the economic and social stations of their parents. Sadly, it took many of my peers thirty or more years to awaken from their trances.

SIGHTING THE PRESENT

How do people not see what surrounds them? How can they not be terrified—horrified—by the outcomes that befell their role models who had earlier chosen to sing the blues? How does one walk through the trash, the needles, the junkies, and the fear—and not see it? Not want to escape it? Not want to scream out? How does one become so inundated with hanging out, getting high, partying, and hustling that he can't consider the possibility of living beyond mere momentary existence? Remarkably, humans are able to acclimate fairly easily to threatening social, economic, and psychological conditions. We are able to tolerate threatening conditions in our daily lives, even when those conditions are horrific. However, when acclimation becomes acquiescence, then self-defeat emerges and the musicians begin to warm up.

𝄞 DA DA DA DA DA

Discerning those who see the futility from those blinded by their poverty is not as difficult as one would suppose. In children, differences between the poverty-bound and the success-bound become manifest at a relatively young age. By ten or eleven years of age, children demonstrate marked differences in social involvement, motivation, and persistence. At this age, I saw school as more valuable than did many of my peers. As I matured, my overriding thoughts were of education and the future. "Just let me reach the next step" was the supplication I repeated daily while studying for tests and applying to schools that would lead to an eventual escape from my surroundings. I was confident that I possessed the motivation and perseverance to succeed. I just had to get in the door.

Tragically, my poverty-bound peers were also trying to access those doors they viewed as important. But toward viable and legitimate spheres of endeavor they demonstrated poor motivation and poor perseverance. My poverty-bound peers accessed their doors through acquiescence to their conditions and self-defeat. Although I was poor economically, my poverty ended there. In motivation, in perseverance, and in vision I was wealthy. For my

poverty-bound peers, economics only set the groundwork for poverty of motivation, poverty of perseverance, and poverty of vision.

Whenever I talked to friends about the desperation and traps we faced and
how to get out, I was rebuked with accusations of wanting to be better than
everyone else. That wasn't my goal at all. I never wanted to outshine my
peers—just my adult role models. I didn't want to be hanging out on the same
street corners doing the same shit twenty-five years later. My friends, on the
other hand, were anxious to ascend to those corners. They were exhilarated to
graduate to the ranks of the rank. They relished hanging out, shooting the shit,
and being cool. You see, even at the tender age of ten, they were poverty bound.

I wanted so badly for my friends to point their lives away from the pits, to
join the journey. But they didn't see street life as pits, they saw it as a sort of rite
of passage. As I entered the tenth grade, they boasted, "Yeah man, I got a
crumb snatcher [baby] by that girl." When I received my high school diploma,
they swaggered, "Yeah, I spent six months in detention for hittin' a cop. Dude
shouldn't have got in my face!" And when I came home on semester break,
they crowed, "Yeah, I quit school. There's mo' money hustlin' on these streets
than bein' some punk-ass college boy." And to my chagrin, no matter how
much I spoke of self-respect, education, and "cashless" values, my words were
lost on the street corners and basketball courts of the neighborhood.

I finally gave up on my neighborhood friends and began to align with individuals who wanted more than the streets. I was just not the same as the homeboys. Even today, when I encounter them on the corners, I find myself different
than the few still alive and not incarcerated or intoxicated. We just have always
seen the world differently. The ones who finally gained sight of the futility
now lament the agony of lost and wasted time, poor priorities, and unconquerable impediments. For the others, I'm still a punk-ass college boy. Near the end
of our conversations, they invariably remark, "Jim, I always knew you were
gonna be something special." I try to tell them they can still get an education
or learn a trade and be something other than a street hustler. For me, this seems
a prudent response. How do I dare tell them I always knew they were going to
be bums?

THE FAMILIARITY OF POVERTY

Unfamiliarity with success serves as the most significant impediment to its attainment. For the greatest part of my journey, I had no clear picture of what I was pursuing or where I would end. I just knew it had to be something and somewhere different than my present surroundings. For me, the unknown future of an educated black man was less frightening than the very certain destiny of black street hustlers. The prospects of the streets terrified me. I guess that made me a punk. Nonetheless, I continued to work hard. Today—still—I am unsure whether my achievements were more a pursuit or an escape. But during my journey, it really didn't matter. I could clearly and without mistake see the desperation around me. So, I decided not to be in the same mire twenty-five years later. I decided not to sing the blues:

$\flat$ DA DA DA DA DA
My momma dear, she was poor as can be,
DA DA DA DA DA
Her man left her here, and the whole family.
DA DA DA DA DA
Ain't no one here I can cry my eyes to,
DA DA DA DA DA
Young, black, and hungry: just what would you do?

Perhaps blindness to what surrounds you is not the problem. Closer to the truth may be an unwillingness to move beyond what is known and what is familiar. People do that which is familiar to them, irrespective of its utility in their lives. Neurotics remain neurotic because it's familiar to them. It's what they know. Depressed persons, angry persons, even confident persons all act in ways consistent with their view of the world. What my friends saw and emulated was what was right there in front of them. Nefarious persons—gangsters, hustlers, pimps, and players—those were their familiar guideposts. Never did my friends seem able to see role models whose lives were more pedestrian. For them, teachers, lawyers, and scientists were indiscernible. Psychologists, engineers, and architects were seemingly beyond their ken and didn't exist. As my friends became increasingly acclimated to their worldview, they became less likely to pursue the unfamiliarity of success.

Familiarity with poverty may actually be reinforcing and binding for poor people because it is what they know. They know and embrace it like a warm blanket—familiar and protecting from the chill of the unknown. People are motivated to maintain a sense of their worlds. They desire to master and know their worlds completely. Such knowledge provides us predictability, and we seem particularly adept at maintaining familiar and predictable worlds. Psychologists use the term *homeostasis* to describe the tendency of people to move toward balance, equilibrium, and predictability in their worlds. That is, people are motivated to avoid lack of balance or the unfamiliar. Homeostasis applied to impoverishment is troublesome because its attainment works against moving out. If you can maintain balance—keep the bills paid, provide food, shelter, and care, and otherwise "get by"—then you are doing all that is required. By "getting by," we achieve homeostasis. Moreover, we don't have to be stressed or bothered by the sacrifices associated with achieving *more*. For many of us, homeostasis is evident in the very words we hear on the streets every day.

Making it or *hanging* or *getting by* is homeostasis. It is familiar and comfortable. It is what poor persons know, and it holds them and prevents them from leaving its familiarity. There lies the problem. Because in order to *become* or to be successful, "making it" and "hanging" and "getting by" must become insufficient. We must stretch beyond homeostasis to be dissatisfied with our present situation. We must be out of equilibrium and out of balance in order to effect change. Disequilibrium is the nature of change—whether physical or mental—in the

---

Scene: YESTERDAY, TODAY, AND TOMORROW
ON THE STREET

John: Hey man, how you doing?
Jerry: Man, I'm just trying to hang. How 'bout you?
John: I'm making it.

universe. I think black people have enjoyed enough equilibrium and home-ostasis. Let's create some turmoil and disequilibrium for our lives and the lives of our children. "Making it" only keeps us tied psychologically to the familiarity of poverty. And that familiarity becomes a song—a song of the blues:

𝄞 DA DA DA DA DA
All 'round me as far, as far as I see,
DA DA DA DA DA
Dirt, crime, and babies, and such poverty.
DA DA DA DA DA
Young kids 'fraid to walk a day in the sun,
DA DA DA DA DA
'Cause Johnny done went and got him a gun.

SIGHTING THE FUTURE

Black people are no longer exclusively the poor persons associated with earlier eras. We are now architects, teachers, and scientists. We have taken advantage of opportunities. We live in suburban homes. We work in professional careers. We strive to give our children bright and promising futures. However, familiarity with an inaccurate image continues to trap and censure a significant portion of our communities. That image is one of rampant and pervasive impoverishment. It affects our worldview and our self-concepts. Those of us who are striving, achieving, and making a life for our families are like a silent minority. We are intimidated by accusations of insensitivity when we are successful. We cringe at the prospect of being labeled Uncle Toms and sellouts, particularly if our success is attained in ways that deviate from traditional—and at some point approved—black fields of endeavor such as athletics and entertainment. And, overwhelmingly, our leadership has further cemented that image of impoverishment into the American psyche. While America and our leaders rally to the aid of the purportedly oppressed, legions of hardworking and achievement-oriented black persons are ignored and, in some cases, chastised. The familiarity of poverty is thereby reinforced through inaccurate images.

Examples of black advancers, well heeled and defiantly unapologetic, run counter to the familiar. Until we reject what is familiar and comfortable and safe, we will continue to fight success. Some of us will continue to correlate black skin with welfare, handouts, and lack of opportunity because it is a song that we know by heart.

We must learn to accept, for our people, both our successes and our failures. Some of us are doing very well, while others of us are not doing well and never will. We *must* accept that. However, to do so means also to accept the ever-increasing improvement of America and its opportunities. Acceptance of such a notion runs so counter to how we see the world that we reject it outright. And by doing so we reject not only America's advancements, but also in some measure our own individual and group advancements. Surely it is far less threatening psychologically to assert lack of opportunity than to accept that The Struggle is nearly over—and, moreover, that by being remiss, we've been left behind. So instead of accepting the possibility of having arrived, we become tragically and psychologically tied to the dogma that *as long as one black person—even one—remains poor, a disproportionate economic relationship exists based upon race and past injustices.* And as a result of maintaining that dogma, we all remain tied—yoked inextricably—to some nebulous and indefinite struggle steeped in the past.

In order to move forward socially, economically, and psychologically, we must throw off the familiarity of poverty. We must accept black successes as more than rarities, isolated instances, and anomalies. As well, we must accept the failures of our race peers without invoking some tired-assed rhetoric. We must stop singing the blues. The theme of "total black success or no success at all" is a hindrance to us as individuals and as a group. It inclines us to believe that black persons who have not made it are irrevocably hamstrung by the system. Moreover, it denies successful black persons their due. Those who are successful continue to be perceived as "the lucky ones," while the rest—the supposed majority—are perceived as inextricable from their economic morass. It suggests that until the black race in its entirety is economically middle class, America will remain a discriminatory hell. Such conceptions often cause me and other Americans to ask, "What do you people want?"

Rather than singing the blues of poverty, it is important to establish standards that will affect the outlooks and lifestyles of your children, grandchildren, great-grandchildren, and their children. They will inherit from you the valuable human assets of motivation and perseverance. They will become intolerant to half-assed, half-stepping, self-pitying, defeatist behaviors and attitudes. If you don't make decisions to affect your life positively, then through your own indifference, decisions will be made for you. Indecision is decision—for yourself and for your children. Failing to exercise choice impoverishes you.

Equality is a double-edged sword. It not only cuts America in its historic treatment of black persons and decries racism, but also cuts a swath in black consciousness. It challenges us to either succeed or fail on our own merits—without excuses, without rationalizations, and without singing the blues—whenever equal opportunity exists.

Chapter 9

IT'S ALL YOUR FAULT
Nah, Nah, Nah, Nah, Nah, Nah

Liberty means responsibility. That is why most men dread it.
—George Bernard Shaw

Only the most intelligent and the most stupid do not change.
—Confucius

Black delayers are simply unwilling to be accountable for their futures. To them, it's always someone else's fault. They use racism, discrimination, and prejudice like shields protecting them from questions related to self-determination and accountability. You couldn't ask for more effective defenses. Who could possibly question that racism, discrimination, and prejudice exist? No one. So black delayers have little problem adopting these shields because little challenge to their use presents itself. And when there is a hint of a challenge, the challenger (if black) is vilified or ostracized from the group, or (if nonblack) is slapped hard and repeatedly with the race card. Delayers, therefore, have their bases covered for their lack of personal responsibility. However, that same coverage of bases keeps them firmly attached to their shields. They cannot allow themselves attempts at success in the system, because if success is achieved then their entire approach and life progression is called into question.

Scene: DINNER CONVERSATION, GRANDMOTHER TO GRANDSON

Barbara: Gerald, I saw you on TV the other day during that protest downtown. Did anything come of that?

Gerald: We held up the morning commute pretty well. I think we got our point across.

Barbara: What's that?

Gerald: That they can't just do what they want to do whenever they want to do it.

Barbara: What'd they try to do, baby?

Gerald: They always tryin' to do something Grandmom. Tryin' to keep us down. I ain't accepting it. Not after all our people done gone through. They forced us over here to be slaves, abused us for hundreds of years, controlled our families and communities, educated us to believe that everything comes through them, beat and incarcerated us in record numbers. And after all that they just want us to forget it. Like it didn't happen. Right. We all just supposed to get along? I don't think so. Let them pay up for what they done.

Moreover, an entire lifestyle adopted and perfected by their parents, peers, friends, and children would melt away. They *must* hold on desperately to their shields. They must delay.

For black delayers, it is exceedingly easy to blame some nebulous source like "the system" for placing obstacles in their paths. This can be done willy-nilly without incurring too significant a threat to one's self-worth. The system is such an enormous entity that opportunities to assign blame are plentiful and readily available. But to look into a mirror—real or imagined—and abdicate personal responsibility for oneself requires more. That cannot be done willy-nilly; it requires a step beyond blame. The individual must accept—in his mind—being vanquished by a system that is purportedly too powerful to be defeated. That is, "the system" must be seen as omnipotent and posed directly in opposition to its victims. Beliefs such as these require a great number of people in agreement. There must exist some sense of collusion with others similarly inclined toward blaming the system. However, systems don't, by themselves, make us lazy, incompetent, or unaccountable. In addition to the perceived omnipotence of the system, there must be some voice or philosophy that emanates from the "victims" that reinforces and acquiesces to lack of personal responsibility—something that is close and personal. I believe that the source of that voice is us. Entitlement—pure and simple—is the philosophy and voice that fuels the engines of black delayers. Through anger at the nation's racial history and frustration regarding a history of unmet promises, they enact their resistance to acclimate. In their minds, the system becomes a perpetual scapegoat—absorbing all their frustrations, validating their delusions of powerlessness, and legitimizing their abdication of personal responsibility.

Consider Cecille: a mother of four—five, if you, like Cecille, count her husband. She has always had a hard way to go. The same things that got in her mother's way now seem to get in her way. It's like an old movie playing over and over. Hell, as far as she knows, it was the same for her grandmother and great grandmother. The world never gave them much of a shot at happiness either. People being prejudiced or racist kept them down. And now it seems the same things are going to keep Cecille down, too. And having no dependable man in the house, never enough money, and too many damned kids don't make it any easier. Generation after generation—if it's not the system keeping them down, then who is?

ADDING OUR FOREBEARS TO THE EQUATION

For many it is very difficult to work harmoniously with the vestiges of the same system that enslaved and abused their forebears. Delayers may actually perceive their resistance and recalcitrance as continuing to fight the good fight: in essence, continuing the spirit of resistance to an oppressive and abusive system.

One need only reference the astronomical costs of the welfare and corrections systems to attest to their drain upon the nation's resources. Some delayers may even see their dependency as part of the revolution—that is, bleeding the oppressor. But black delayers are in error for a number of reasons. First, systems rarely change as a result of outside influences. They are too big and self-perpetuating to do so. When the system is as large and multifaceted as a nation, black delayers and their delaying tactics can be effectively ignored. And isn't that what is increasingly happening now? Delayers have been relegated largely to a refuse pile. They have become ineffectual, laughable, and as bothersome as gnats. Only minor distractions in the progression of the nation's life. Their ability to effect change in the system is negligible. No one cares if they pout. Changes come from a combination of factors that emanate from both inside and outside a system's boundaries. So their waging of war from the outside is doomed to fail.

Second, delayers are in essence waging a war of attrition. By definition, such campaigns are long and protracted. After some passage of time people typically forget what exactly it is they are warring for. We already have a case in point. Our children are removed from the history of race relations in this country. Just ask them questions about Angela Davis, Stokley Carmichael, A. Philip Randolph, Elijah Muhammad, and others. Perhaps you yourself are not quite familiar with the significance of these people's contribution. That makes my point. While we wait in our war of attrition, the true meaning of what we're waiting for gets lost. That is, are we now warring for civil rights, or equal protection under the law, or reparations, or something else? Or has the war ended?[1]

Lastly, resistance and entrenchment in the end does not engender positive and cooperative reactions from the system. Rather, it engenders feelings of ill will that do little to improve relations between groups in this country. These feelings arise and present as particularly resistant to change. Whether through the depletion of funding sources and programs or through the rise of neo-Nazi groups, feelings of ill will are created as people tire of the recalcitrance and entitlement of delayers. Ultimately, the philosophies and traditions advanced by black delayers only add to longstanding miscommunication between groups.

The mistake we advancers too often make is extending unconditional love to these delayers. Because they are black, and because of our history, and because of the system, we give them sway. Rather than holding them to a standard that demands responsibility for intergenerational advancement or failure, we cut them a break. That unconditional love is precisely what flies back into our faces because the recipients become entitled, scoffing whenever we presume that they bear some of the weight for their lives.

Whenever we presume to hold them minimally responsible for their outcomes, black delayers respond, "C'mon, can't you show me some love?"

Speaking for myself, other black advancers, and our forebears: *No!*

Chapter 10

BAA, BAA, BLACK SHEEP
Black Leaders and Their Windmills

Philosophy is perfectly right in saying that life must be understood backward.
But then one forgets the other clause—that it must be lived forward.
—SØREN KIERKEGAARD

People, like sheep, tend to follow a leader—occasionally in the right direction.
—ALEXANDER CHASE

Don Quixote has always been an interesting character to me. While all around him the world was changing, he stood steadfastly in the past, flailing at romantic visions. An anachronism personified, Quixote permitted his dreams and worldview to cement him to the past. In large part, the same can be said of black leadership today. I find much of current black leadership sadly out of touch with the present-day needs of black Americans. These leaders—and their unconsidered, ill-fated followers—are entrenched and clichéd by the 1960s—out of step with the demands of American society at this juncture in time. Our leaders march blithely to a beat that has lost its measure.

Their now-antiquated strategies and philosophies were most useful when civil rights were at the fore of black consciousness and struggles. Then, as a people, we were a monolith of thwarted and unattained dreams. Then, the battle scheme of the 1960s was functional. We needed to march, to protest, to riot, and to engage in other methods of resistance. However, the strategies and philosophies that defined those civil rights efforts now seem as relics from a hallowed past. Sit-ins, accusations of racism, protest marches, and the performance of rhetoric-laden speeches have become antiquated. Exhausted and atrophied, their power to influence and effect change has long been dissipated.

These relics are dusted off and, in a perfunctory, almost obligatory fashion, resuscitated whenever some injustice occurs. And sadly, despite their impotence, many of us still rise to the call to arms. Familiarity, rather than efficacy, motivates us. Who could ever forget the oldies but goodies: The words to "We Shall Overcome," the slogans "Power to the People" and "Say it Loud," and the self-handicapping rationalization that the white man is the root of all our problems?

We are no longer a monolith of thwarted and unattained dreams. Many advancers do not believe that marching is the most effective avenue to change. They neither feel the need to march nor care to watch the marchers limp by. Today, civil rights have become (and rightfully so) a secondary or tertiary concern for many black persons. For them, economic, political, and social advancement have been realized. The promise of upward mobility has displaced the obliqueness of civil rights. With good schools, jobs, homes, and futures attainable, getting into corporate boardrooms and desirable neighborhoods have, for many, supplanted marches, sit-ins, and rhetoric.

While the majority of black Americans has increasingly identified with success philosophies, black leaders often still cast their lot with the strugglers of the community. They take up the cause of the disenfranchised—the purported victims of discrimination and racism. This strategy made sense when the vast majority of black Americans were poor, with little or no access to avenues of success. However, during the last forty years or so, black Americans have enjoyed unprecedented successes. Unfortunately, much of that success has been attained without the assistance of our leaders. While advancers have adjusted to new social, economic, and political contingencies, our leaders (e.g., Rev. Jesse Jackson, Minister Louis Farrakhan, Rev. Al Sharpton) have been found ill prepared to change with the prevailing winds.

Nowhere is their quixotic perspective more evident than in the area of economics. Championing the causes of the poor, they have habitually ignored the needs of the well heeled. While our leaders lament the dramas of the purported masses, advancers press on. As revealed in the nation's most recent census, black Americans have reached new all-time highs in median income. Additionally, the number of black Americans represented in the highest income level has increased sixfold in the last twenty years.[1]

It's true. *Accept it!* These winners have identified with the American Dream and are pursuing it with a relentless fervor. Moreover, they have established a pattern of success for their families. Likely, their children will—as the children from other ethnic and racial groups do—continue that legacy of success.

Yet despite these statistics and an increasingly good prognosis for black Americans, much of the country (and the world) continues to identify with black strugglers and stragglers: the delayers. Worse, black losers are inordinately associated with the economic and social stature of black communities. Gang members, drug addicts, criminals, the undereducated, the chronically poor, and the refuse of our communities garner the attention of the nation's media and black leaders. Our leaders voice their concern for the strugglers—and sometimes the losers—of our communities, while largely spurning upwardly mobile persons.[2]

And, until very recently, black middle-class persons remained quiet, intimidated by charges of not really being black. Their achievements and successes were often viewed as antithetical to what was considered real when discussing "the black experience." For realizing the very same achievements and successes that our forebears fought so desperately to have, upwardly mobile black persons traditionally have been largely ignored by whites as atypical and reviled by blacks as having sold out to "the man."

This inattention toward upwardly mobile black persons emanates out of the very spheres from which our leaders emerge. Historically, black churches played an integral role in providing leadership for our communities. Their Christian-based philosophies espoused embracing the downtrodden, the meek inheriting the earth, and the reversal of the fortunes of the greatest and the least in the afterlife. Such notions were probably quite attractive to an oppressed people. And black people, heartened by acceptance in the eyes of a god more powerful than their oppressors, looked to the church for leadership. I suppose they concluded that if one is to board a ship, then who better at the helm than God or God's messenger. They had only to be good and obedient— and *patient*! Such teachings also effectively served the interests of slaveholders who were more interested in passivity and submission than souls. Many slaveholders insisted that their human property attend church services. Even they understood the notion of religion as a potential opiate.

While many of us relished being embraced and patient, more well-heeled and venturesome black persons continued to strive—quietly and diligently. They refused to be sedated by the anesthesia of a better afterlife or the perpetual black struggle. Even today, upwardly mobile black persons are rarely sedate in their quest for present-world rewards. They have been—and continue to be—aggressive and relentless in their objectives. Outwardly and inwardly they have been keen in identifying, pursuing, and attaining goals. And for that keenness, they have been largely neglected in the consideration of black leaders. While dedicated to uplifting a people, our leaders have historically been wantonly remiss in the embracing of the self-willed.

Ironically, upward mobility has been one of the very important goals of the civil rights movement. Its attainment, however, is often followed by repudiation. Those who do well are often considered outside the community or peripheral to it. For their industry, advancers are perceived as "the lucky ones" who distance themselves from their brethren while forgetting from where they came. To many persons inside and outside black communities, this neglect implies that only those who are struggling economically, socially, and politically are *truly* black. Only they are deserving of the efforts of black leaders. And according to those who tie civil rights to religion, only they deserve to sit in the pews of righteousness. The well heeled are assumed not destined to receive rewards in the afterlife, for they certainly aren't downtrodden. And they definitely aren't meek and waiting to inherit the earth. They dare to enjoy the good life now.

This neglect of upwardly mobile black persons was not as glaring a problem thirty or forty years ago as it is today. But, rather suddenly, America is faced with *legions* of black persons who are in the middle and upper classes. Economically, the legions of the downtrodden are dwindling. One would have

hoped that the perspective of black leaders would have changed as their followers became increasingly less meek, less afterlife oriented, and less willing to
wait for their inheritance of the earth. However, on the whole, black leaders
who are steeped in traditional church values have not changed. They continue
to attend differentially to the downtrodden and the well heeled. This differential attention, as much as anything, has contributed to the rift between middle-
class black persons and those black persons who continue to struggle.[3]

Fortunately, a new breed of black preachers has emerged. They present as
more aware and attentive to the needs of their congregations. Their political
activism (a longstanding expectation and tradition for black religious leaders)
also includes a fairly aggressive awareness and approach. Here-and-now issues
as well as attainment of pursuits beyond basic human rights have become part
of their mission. For that change in philosophy they are to be commended. But
for those preachers who remain steeped in traditional black church values, a
barely passing grade is assigned. They are no longer leaders of the black community at large, but purveyors of old-time sentiments. Their quixotic lack of
response to changes in the world serves only to contribute to a sense of endear-
ment for delayers and a sense of estrangement for advancers.

This is not to suggest that religion and traditional preachers have been
wholly divisive to black people. To the contrary, traditional preachers have
wielded significant power in local and national politics to the benefit of black
persons as we sought basic human rights in this country. By invoking God,
understanding, meekness, and brotherhood, black leaders have been able to
garner the support of strugglers. Moreover, they gained the support of non-
blacks who wanted to further the successes of the flock. So both traditional
and new-breed preachers have had a significant influence as leaders of black
Americans. Still, the preponderance of church persons in leadership roles for
black communities has been disturbing.

Black persons—qualified and inclined to lead—from secular arenas have
enjoyed little access to political spheres. Their influence has been negligible
when compared to that of *the preachers*. Generally, they have been unable to
command the large following that those who seem to know God personally
have. They are rarely recognized by us—or them—as representing anything

more than the fringe. In the hearts of black folks and in the minds of others, preachers have always been the recognized leaders of the community.

In my opinion, it is way past time for us to look away from leaders defined by church involvement. It is bothersome when some joker in a robe implies that he or she can speak for me and for millions of other black Americans. I am bothered by their audacity and by a media that foists them upon us as shepherds. The same can be said of the major national so-called black-oriented organizations. The National Association for the Advancement of Colored People, the National Urban League, and the Southern Christian Leadership Conference, for example, have enjoyed a rich history in their advocacy of the needs of black people. They have been helpful in the upward mobility of some black persons. Today, however, they are increasingly ill equipped to address the multifarious nature of black opinions, needs, and aspirations. They—along with the preachers—are increasingly unaware of the pulse of black America, not because they misread the pulse, but because there are countless pulses. No one philosophical outlook will address them all.

I daresay black leaders and organizations always have been unable to represent all black persons. No single perspective can possibly address all the subgroups that make up black Americans, or any other group. Up to very recent times, dissenters have been labeled as Uncle Toms by both black and white persons. Such admonitions are no longer tenable. There are far too many voices rising in dissent. Many of them don't need or want leaders, particularly ones who are entrenched in the past.

Few upwardly mobile black persons feel the need to be led. They have "become" through their own emotional and constitutional wherewithal. Their achievements occur despite the censure of their peers and the silence of black leaders. They might reasonably reject the notion of being led like herd animals. They might reject being shepherded in their thoughts and deeds. Free to make their own decisions and chancing success or failure, they may be the only ones among us who are truly free. Unfortunately, in the minds of many, it is more comfortable to be led. By letting others make our decisions or control our actions, responsibility for any possible failure is avoided. And who better to entrust one's present and future with than God?

That black people need leaders is a proposition to which I remain wholly unconvinced. The idea is a terribly racist and delimiting one. It implies that "the people" (one may substitute flock, children, pickaninnies, slaves) need to be led. Apparently, black individuals are assumed not capable of forging their own lives devoid of leadership or community consciousness; we must be led. And, laughingly, it is our preachers who must do the leading: Father Divine, Minister Malcolm X, Rev. Dr. Martin Luther King Jr., Minister Louis Farrakhan, Rev. Al Sharpton, Rev. Jesse Jackson, Reverend Ike, Daddy Grace, and thousands of local emissaries. If black communities must have leaders, then it is crucially important that the helms be influenced by a variety of navigators. Politicians, social scientists, lawyers, economists, and—yes—even an occasional preacher should be part of the navigation crew. Otherwise, we are largely destined and restricted to follow one invariant, unalterable, and limiting course.

Chapter 11

IS YOU THE ONE?
Saving Your Own Damned Self

This generation had no [Frederick] Douglass, no [Adam Clayton] Powell, no [Martin Luther] King, no Malcolm [X] to break things down for them.
—SUSAN TAYLOR

People who stand on the corners doing nothing might as well be dead. They're just taking up space. They don't have a purpose or anything. They're just there.
—MILTON PITTMAN

At one time in our history whenever a black child was born the words, "Is You the One?" would be uttered. In essence: Are you *the* child who will one day lead our people—millions of souls—out of bondage, despair, and oppression? One hell of a burden to put on a kid still sticky from the birth process. "Is You the One?" reinforces waiting, biding our time, and maintaining homeostasis until we are delivered by our leader.

The journey toward freedom for black people probably began as soon as the first black persons were sold and loaded onto ships bound for the Americas. Freedom has been—and continues to be—a battle cry for black Americans. In that journey toward freedom, we have largely turned to our leaders for direction. Sojourner Truth, Malcolm X, A. Philip Randolph, Martin Luther

King Jr., and Elijah Muhammad were people who had the group's interests at heart even at the expense of their lives and personal safety.

On our long journey toward freedom, our leaders have evoked in us strong feelings of racial identity and racial unity—in essence, a staunch tribalism of sorts. However, that tribalism has been racially oppressive and in the service of squelching individuality. Dissent, long valued and central in our resistance to oppressive conditions, has been notoriously disrespected and discouraged in our relations among ourselves. We have been a flock bunched together toward a purportedly common purpose, not a coalition of individuals with varied opinions. Historically, we have been largely an aimless herd in wait for our shepherd. And we are in constant anticipation of who will next be the One.

A number of devastating outcomes befall us while waiting for the One. Those outcomes—lack of personal responsibility, resignation to one's current circumstances, and undermining of self-efficacy and self-determination—affect us on both individual and community levels. While waiting, we individually become firmly entrenched in cycles of rationalization and apathy. Much time is spent explaining away our lack of industry or seeking out similarly compromised others who will support us in our morass. Without missing a beat, our children learn the very same behaviors through the models we provide. Communities are built on such foundations and remain in such states for generations.

Those very same attributes—accountability, motivation, and self-determination—most closely tied with success in this country are, over time, increasingly compromised while waiting for the One. Now, just for a moment, think of the worst among us. It doesn't matter whether it's Pookie, Tamika, June Bug, or some trifling stranger you see on the street every day. What crucial attributes are found wanting? The presumption that everyone is motivated to do well through their own self-determination is flawed from the beginning. Some of us are simply unmotivated to take charge of our lives. Some of us are simply unwilling to be accountable for our futures. Some of us would rather wait.

While waiting, one only maintains, gets by, and hangs in there, while each day hoping the One will appear on the horizon. I believe that waiting for the One is most likely a self-esteem protection strategy. While waiting, delayers don't challenge in any significant fashion the status quo. That way, they can avoid the potentially negative feedback that people (namely, advancers) who challenge the system risk everyday. One can, as my Philadelphia homies are apt to say, "lay in the cut and just chill"—while awaiting deliverance.

Delayers will no doubt take exception to the use of the "Is You the One?" analogy. They might cite its age and outdatedness. They might be correct. But "Is You the One?" is only an allegory. Whether you term it "Is You the One?" or "Giving Back to the Community" or "We Need Strong Leaders," they all represent the same thing: to wit, that some one person—or some multiplicity of persons—should be charged with saving their raggedy asses. Can't you just see those who choose to *wait*? Positioned deep in a pit—dead weight—feet dragging, arms open upward like an eighteen-month-old reaching desperately for that hand up.

How do you stop waiting for the One and learn to save yourself? First, you must recognize that your life is your own. It belongs not to your parents or your church—and most assuredly not to the black community at large. It's your life! Yours! This concept will probably be the most difficult to internalize and enact, because we black persons have been indoctrinated through our history, our leaders, our communities, and our nation that we are *family*. And as family we feel obligated to our racial brothers and sisters, our history, and our communities. Second, realizing that your life is your own is fraught with the terror of self-determinism. That is, it's now up to you. No excuses. No rationalizations. No blame. You. Just you and your character. Third, taking responsibility for yourself removes you from the safety of numbers. No longer is there a *we* that demands or waits to be addressed. Only you and the mirror remain. Set goals, achieve them, and leave those who refuse to do so behind—*waiting*.

Having attained our physical freedom some time ago, we no longer have to wait for the One. In fact, the One is inside each of us individually. We have been so engrossed in the task of freedom for the entirety of our race that the idea of individual and personal freedom has been disgracefully neglected and often vilified as traitorous. When one considers the possibility of attaining complete freedom for oneself—individually and without the refuse of our communities—psychological conflicts arise. How can I leave my people behind? How dare I disengage and pursue my own total personal freedom? What of those persons I leave behind?

To attain emotional and psychological freedom from the effects of history, oppression, culture, and community, one must take an individual journey. Psychological freedom is idiosyncratic. It cannot be realized en masse. We must recognize that deliverance from physical chains is only one way of being free. Freedom is both physical and mental, but mostly mental. We are a free people. Now, let's be free persons—with psyches, egos, selves, and souls beyond race.

INVICTUS

Out of the night that covers me,
Black as the Pit from pole to pole,
I thank whatever gods may be
For my unconquerable soul.

In the fell clutch of Circumstance
I have not winced nor cried aloud.
Under the bludgeonings of Chance
My head is bloody, but unbowed.

Beyond this place of wrath and tears
Looms but the Horror of the shade,
And yet the menace of the years
Finds, and shall find me, unafraid.

It matters not how strait the gate,
How charged with punishments the scroll,
I am the master of my fate:
I am the captain of my soul.

—William Ernest Henley

Chapter 12

TICKETS TO THE
NEW MINSTREL SHOWS

They will never let me play a part in which a Negro is on top.
  —PAUL ROBESON

I'd walk a million miles for one of your smiles,
My Mammy!
  —"MY MAMMY"

Unquestionably, the donning of blackface is considered the most offensive image of black Americans. Popularized in the 1870s, its theatrical presentation was practiced to portray black Americans in glaringly stereotypic fashion—buffoons not ever to be taken seriously. Negroes were only black-skinned and white-lipped stooges, dancing and singing to the delight of joyfully endorsing audiences. Black Americans had only recently experienced the first phase of freedom: delivery from slavery. A sense of industry, motivation, and self-directedness "among the darkies" was perceived as threatening to our nation's social and economic order. Stereotypic portrayals were often designed to assure both white audiences and potential black advancers of the ineffectuality of these newly freed slaves.

Today, black Americans are experiencing another phase of freedom. Only recently delivered from our second phase of freedom—the common battle for civil rights—we are now free in a different way: free to lay down our battle gear, free to disengage from the group, and free to develop and advance on our own individual merits. Now, in reaction to this third phase of freedom, minstrel shows have reemerged.

Fascinatingly, those original minstrel show audiences have been supplanted by black Americans who now joyfully endorse the buffoonery of our modern-day black clowns. Although dead long ago, it now seems the revivalists of blackface are the black great-great-grandchildren of the slaves, pickaninnies, and sharecroppers originally portrayed: Tyler Perry's Big Momma, in her flower-print muumuu, wielding totalitarian maternal power; Cordozar Broadus's Snoop Dogg, bouncing to aggrandize dangerous but ultimately ineffectual black males; and Jamie Foxx's Wanda from *In Living Color* dominating way too much space with her sassy black female attitude and gargantuan booty. These and countless other portrayals all play to modern-day stereotypes of black life. Black actors, comedians, musicians, and others often adopt these vaudevillian portrayals, buck dancin' and grinnin' all the live-long day.[1]

Black people in blackface appear to address individual and community homeostatic needs. People are often uncomfortable with change. Change can be very hard, very threatening, and very challenging. Change takes us out of our comfort zones. People do that which is familiar to them. This truism has been the bedrock of psychology and clinical intervention. We are not only creatures of habits developed through long histories of reinforcement and conditioning, but we are, moreover, creatures of familiarity. We bristle at changes at home, at work, and in relationships, and may find ourselves moving away from new perspectives and gravitating toward old, familiar ways and means.

Relatedly, in the face of momentous social and historical change, unprecedented opportunities, and stellar achievements for black Americans, blackface portrayals and productions are increasing in frequency. And profitably! Entertainers are raking in millions of dollars providing people with these familiar—but terribly stereotypic—images. There exists a reinforcing familiarity to these stereotypes, and parts of our community endeavor to maintain them. Such entertainment vehicles—whether plays, videos, novels, or films—are minstrel shows, changed simply in cast. Standing in for Shiftless, Lazy, Simpleminded

Negro is No-Good Dog Black Man. Appearing for Strong, Silent, Enduring Negress is Sassy, Loud, Head-Swiveling, Bootie-Shaking Sister. Representing Simpleminded, Quiet, Powerful Buck is Brooding, Angry, Potentially Dangerous Black Man. And for Mammy: Big Momma.

Interestingly, it used to be that blackface was for the entertainment and elevating of white audiences. However, a very significant change has occurred: Black people have joined in the maintenance and perpetuation of racial stereotypes. Their reasons differ, but their messages remain identical: reduction and squelching of the range and variability of black people, their thoughts, their attitudes, and their endeavors.

"Girlfriend can't even dance."
"Brother can't even hoop."
"She ain't got no ass."
"You sound white."
"I'm a pimp/player up in here."
"She's whitewashed."
"I'm getting my mack on."

Perhaps the recent proliferation of these stereotypic depictions has a purpose—albeit poor spirited. New minstrel shows may serve to bolster the self-worth of black delayers as they—and the world—witness increasing numbers of black advancers breaking battle ranks. Ironically, one of the very basic goals of the civil rights movement was the moving away from stereotypes, away from reduction of our personhood and toward an identity not defined by race. Our black forebears tried to demonstrate that black people were more than what white people wanted us to be. Moreover, they tried to demonstrate that we could and would contribute significantly to society and lead in its progress. Now, new minstrel shows are set to thwart those efforts by heaving us back into *black*.

I refuse to give the minstrel players, their producers, or their audiences credit of any kind. Friends have taken me to task about this issue. Generally, they proffer two arguments. First, they argue that we should be happy that these minstrel players are in positions to be seen. They argue, "Well, there was a time you never saw somebody black on television or on stage making big money." I usually counter with the age of that argument. It is time worn: uttered back in the '60s and '70s. It's a remnant from the days of blaxploitation films, when few nonstereotypic roles were available to black actors. But, just as our days of exclusively playing pimps, whores, and mack-daddies are over, so too should be our days of buffoon-grinnin', bootie-shaking, and rump-hoisting. The second argument is that stereotypic portrayals are only enter-tainment, helping us to learn to laugh at ourselves and reminisce about the good old days. "Hey, those folks are entertaining," they assert. "It doesn't really hurt anything." If you believe that, then ask any black child concentrating on her books and her future. Ask her what words and reactions she gets from black and white students alike when she confesses that she doesn't dance, or isn't cool, or doesn't know the name of the latest hip-hop star. Likely, she is met with derision, ridicule, and assaults upon her black character. I and my aca-demic peers suffered the same indignities more than thirty years ago. I would daresay that those exceedingly few black advancers who were available to teach and role model for us also were subjected to questions about their own identi-ties from self-appointed curators of black culture.

I would argue that the messages of minstrel players—then and now—are destructive to the world's perception of us and to the development of identity for ourselves and for our children. Because when I and my sons don't grin, don't buck dance, and don't consider careers as pimps, we are eyed askance by all groups for not being "black enough." The old days, as I remember them, weren't that damn good to begin with. So why the desire to reenact? I, for one, don't try to spend a lot of time rehashing or revisiting painful eras in my life. How 'bout you?

It saddens me to think advancement and progression away from black stereotypes are threatening to our psyches. Part of this is not our fault. The reinforcement and conditioning of oppression has been long and sordid. But so what? I don't care whose fault it is. What are we going to do now?

I believe that as a people, black Americans are in search of identity. We are frightened by the prospect of seeing black in our mirrors but not in our souls. This is particularly the case when one considers that there exist no guidelines for being a black human. We've been guided by our masters, our overseers, our preachers, and our leaders, but little by ourselves. One must remember that for many years we were considered less than human. We are pretty well versed in being black and poor, or black and struggling, or even black and advancing. How now do we embrace black and human?

My contention is that the *black* part doesn't need to be practiced. Melanin is biology, unalterable and definitive. Black culture—partly historical and partly contrived—is an awfully poor guide to development of an individual self.[2]

But irrespective of history or contrivance, blackness represents limits that constrict one's humanity. Hey, I have an idea! Instead of worrying about maintaining my blackness, your blackness, and our blackness, let's explore and expand ourselves in any damned way we want. Let yourself be whatever and whomever you want: free and adaptable. Be what you want. Marry whomever you want. Believe what you will. Behave as you desire. Because when the time comes for you to die, all those who restrict you now will not be able to hand you another life to live as your own. It will be *you* dying. So live as you will, because no matter what you do, it is likely good for you in particular, and good for America—black and otherwise—in general. Your freedom contributes to all our evolving identities and freedoms. Do not regress to familiar stereotypes and images. Let the minstrels dance and sing. Theirs is a song and dance of desperation. They are trying to revive a body that is increasingly nearing death. Don't join them in the resuscitation. Let the old bastard die.

If you desire to be an engineer, then go to school and hang with engineers—and not just black ones. If music is your forte, then join with musicians, ones who know more than rhythm and blues. We must learn how to let others like us be free and reinforce freedom in ourselves and others. Freedom today means being unattached, unencumbered, and unfettered by the quest to balance black community needs with personal goals and beliefs.

On the surface, the black community may feign appreciation for its advancers and dissenters, but these progressives are strangers to us. We don't know them. They challenge us and scare us—every day uncomfortably stretching the range and variability of *black*. The recent proliferation of black theatrical productions, increasing popularity of black music videos, and explosion of black "girlfriend" novels attest to the psychological importance of maintaining that which is familiar, no matter how insulting or degrading. Many of these present-day entertainment vehicles are steeped in stereotypic lore. These portrayals are painful, but it's a pain we know.

With numbers of black advancers increasing, one should expect the continued resurgence of minstrel shows. I contend that as black individuals continue to gravitate toward new, unfettered identities, community defense mechanisms such as minstrel shows will continue to emerge.

Chapter 13

THERE BUT FOR THE GRACE OF GOD GO I

(and Other Lunacy)

If God were suddenly condemned to live the life which he has inflicted upon men, he would kill himself.
—ALEXANDRE DUMAS

Luck is what happens when preparation meets opportunity.
—DARRELL ROYAL

"There but for the grace of God go I" is probably one of the more confounding statements encountered by black persons who have recently ascended from the depths of poverty. All of us are well aware of the significance of religion in the history of black Americans. For centuries many of our forebears swore by God and religion. In those times when it seemed that all was against them, they entrusted their fates and those of their families to the beneficence of these powers. They hoped (nay, prayed) that competing powers (e.g., evil, the devil, the man) would be somehow thwarted from negatively affecting their fates. And for many monumental trials and overwhelming challenges their hopes and prayers were realized.

However, for at least the last forty years or so, realities have changed. Not all has been against us. Although at times faced with much resistance, our

Scene: TY-RAY (A FUTURE ADVANCER),
SITTING IN HIS GRANDMA'S KITCHEN

Ty-Ray: Finally! I applied at least a thousand times and finally I got accepted to that trade school. It's the best in the city. I don't know why I had to go through all them changes with those people.

Grandma: Maybe it just wasn't your time yet, baby. The Lord works in mysterious ways.

Ty-Ray: Well anyway, I'm in. I'm in! They even gave me a tuition waiver.

Grandma: See. Maybe you'd had got in before, but they wouldn't had no money for you. And God knows we ain't had 'nuf money to send you, boy. You see Ty-Ray, my Lord, He works in mysterious ways.

Ty-Ray: I sure wish Tyrone down the street had got in too. We could have studied together. He applied, but he didn't get accepted.

Grandma: That's too bad, baby. But, maybe it wasn't *his* time. The Lord works in mysterious ways.

Ty-Ray: Now I got to worry 'bout how to get down there by six-thirty every morning. Buses don't even start running out there 'til seven.

Grandma: Don't worry, baby. The Lord will find a way.

efforts have nonetheless resulted in forward movement. God and religion notwithstanding, we have achieved in spectacular fashion.

I—and many people just like me—am accomplished because I busted my butt to get there. It had little to do with luck, divine intervention, aligning of the stars, or voodoo. I got there by hard work. The powers that be get little credit. It is my contention that reliance on destiny and forces greater than ourselves retard our efforts toward psychological freedom. We become minions of those powers rather than titans of life's progression. For those who align with the grace of God perspective, future success or failure as well as psychological health or illness are presumed beyond one's personal power. As a natural consequence of such thinking, critical footings for launching and sustaining a high quality of life are disregarded. Rather, a high quality of life is viewed as serendipitous—lucky, unforeseen, and unearned.

Delayers, for example, too often throw up their hands and relinquish their sense of efficacy and self-determination to "forces more powerful than themselves." They then beseech the powers that be for guidance and deliverance for their lives. God and devil, mercy and evil, resignation and self-reliance, and the man are variously seen as forces that intervene, to their advantage or disadvantage, in life events. If the intervention is to their advantage, then delayers see themselves—and are seen by others—as very fortunate. That is, God picked them out for success, and they are supposed to consider themselves blessed—and highly favored. If, however, the intervention is to their disadvantage, then they're not so fortunate. They were forsaken by God or somehow the devil got involved and put his two cents in. They are therefore not blessed—and, presumably, only moderately or lowly favored. God is even more intricately involved when it comes to failure. Failures are the person's fault, while successes are God's work. And at those times when some celestial assistance could have been useful but was not forthcoming, God didn't think the person could handle success yet!

Of course, such thinking is steeped in our community's intimate connection to religion. Lack of power and efficacy evoke familiar, and thereby comfortable, images of our days of struggle. Then, back in those days, we put ourselves in Jesus's hands because our own hands had so little power to effect change. Although no longer slaves, we are inheritors through our fables of an enslaved outlook. As a result, we still seem to overidentify with our historic, although now changeable and conquerable, powerlessness. Despite hard-fought battles for power, efficacy, and self-determination, delayers still insist it's the grace of God and look beseechingly to the few fortunate ones to save the rest of us.

Far too many of us still believe that things—powerful things—outside our-selves are poised to determine our destiny. Whether it's god, the devil, mercy, evil, the lucky ones, the system, the white man, or a host of other idols doesn't matter. What does matter is that we almost joyfully relinquish our power of self-determination while awaiting the rapture or the blues. The grace of God per-spective even causes some black advancers to assume patron status for the unlucky ones. They, too, become swayed and entrapped by the romanticism of the past. The notion, "You're one of the lucky ones and you've been blessed," hangs like a sword of Damocles over the heads of these entranced black advancers. Statements such as, "How were you able to get out?" "What made you different?" and "Everyone can't be as smart as you," serve to further cement the presumed connection between black advancers and the unlucky ones.[1]

LUCKY OR DUPED

Being presumed to be one of the lucky ones negates my personal efforts and struggles. Rather, I am cast as a representative of the race—one of the lucky ones among the masses. That casting yokes me psychologically to the larger community. The lucky ones—almost by definition—are pressed with the expectation to help those not as fortunate. What an absolute snow job! Worse, the unlucky ones—enabled by religious heritage and encouraged by a largely God-fearing community—need only wait until their representatives return to uplift them. Such thinking runs rampant and largely unchecked among the unlucky ones. But, more important, such thinking has served to haunt and hamstring the lucky ones for more than a century.

I'm not particularly smart. I work hard. That's all. But because I am an accomplished professional, I am—according to black delayers—supposed to remain humble because some of us were not *lucky* enough to have the advan-tages that I had. I was, in their eyes, fortunate and blessed. I am supposed to be humbled by the greatness of forces more powerful than me. In my opinion, this all implies lack of efficacy and self-direction: that is, some deity—consistent with and perpetuating of our community's religious heritage—had a hand in my ascension. Worse, it implies rationalization: that is, if you happen not to be chosen as one of the lucky ones, then you can't be blamed for your lack of effort. It's up to the lucky ones to uplift you.

Perhaps it is my idiosyncratic thinking, but it all reminds me very much of the theories related to the makers of the pyramids of Egypt. There are a goodly number of persons, including some recent filmmakers, who find it more plausible that spaceships traveled millions of miles, landed on the Giza Plateau, and fashioned the pyramids than to consider that maybe Africans completed this mighty feat. That is, they'd rather believe little bubble-headed extraterrestrials had a hand in building the pyramids before considering that conception, design, and completion was accomplished by people with brown skin.

Similarly, some persons find it more reasonable to posit that forces greater than ourselves had a hand in the success of selected black Americans than to consider that through self-determination, self-reliance, and a drive toward excellence these people controlled their own lives and achievements. In other words, some persons would rather endorse the fairy tale of the "lucky ones" than consider that every black American of relatively average intelligence is capable of achieving whatever they wish with a bit of fortitude. And, moreover, in appreciation of their good fortune, these lucky ones are now charged with coming back to the community with their knowledge to help uplift the masses. That's the deal they get for their good fortune. Dependence of the masses, it would seem, is much more palatable than their empowerment.

I believe such thinking is at the root of our "Give Back to the Community" folly. And I believe that is why so many who are waiting to be given back to are so very angry. In their opinion, black advancers are reneging on the deal. What black delayers fail to realize is that black advancers were never part of the deal to begin with. We never sat down with delayers at the Table of Unchallenged Destiny, so many of us don't feel obligated to play out that hand with you. We were reared in the same communities and were dealt the same initial cards, but we've played at different tables. The Tables of Hard Work, Perseverance, Long-Term Goals, and Intergenerational Advancement are where we placed our bets. And for those bets we got new cards—education, efficacy, and direction. Where did you place your bets?

We're playing our hands. And winning! Would you like to play a hand at our tables, or stand pat?

BROTHER, CAN YOU SPARE A DIME?

Why would any person assume that everyone who grew up in the 'hood would be motivated to give back? Many black advancers were subjected to daily physical, emotional, and psychological dangers while surviving there. Many of us were often unsupported and reviled by our peers—and sometimes by our role models. Some of us even had to toil alone—uncertain where we were heading, but resolute about where we desired *not* to be. Given that history, is it now easier to see why some black advancers don't rush back to the community? It's not that they don't want to be black. It's because they want you to work hard to orchestrate your own life without rationalizations. It's because they don't want to encourage dependency, but desire to foster among you self-sufficiency and self-efficacy. After all the effort and sacrifice, and after all the poor support and ridicule, are black advancers now to believe the "there but for the grace of God" philosophy? Are we now to feel humble and lucky? And based on such an erroneous philosophy, are we now obligated to give back to the community? Ha!

I would argue that the issue is not whether black advancers give back to the community. Of course giving back is done. It's just not in the form that black Americans have been trained to receive. It is not dependence-based. This criterion, more than any other, black advancers will insist upon. We will not encourage dependency. You will not get a handout. It ain't coming. Stop looking for it.

What is truly unfortunate and gets ignored is the fact that no group gives back to the black community more than black advancers. Every single day and in myriad ways, black advancers give back. Just by being in spheres where black Americans not too long ago were excluded is giving back. Kicking obstacles from your path is giving back. Encouraging you to join our ranks is giving back.

We advancers will continue to clear roads for you, point to the direction toward success, and even whisper to you where the pitfalls exist. But we will not under any circumstances turn around, come back down that road, pick you up, hoist you onto our shoulders, and carry your ass down the road. Our encouragement and modeling of self-sufficiency without dependency is the best you can hope for.

You're welcome.

Chapter 14

COO! COO! PIGEONHOLES ARE FOR THE BIRDS

PREJUDICE, n. A vagrant opinion without visible means of support.
　—AMBROSE BIERCE, *THE DEVIL'S DICTIONARY*

The dust of exploded beliefs may make a fine sunset.
　—GEOFFREY MADAN

used to become irritated by people who attempted to limit my personal psychological freedom and development. I found them trying to pigeonhole me into how they thought black males should be. They wanted me silent and sullen. But I wasn't. They wanted me uncultured and weak minded. But I wasn't. They wanted me dangerous, but ultimately ineffectual. But I wasn't. I believe the antithesis—arrogance?—represented in me caused them some disturbance. For them, I spoke too well. I had too much education. I knew too much and I was a bit too self-assured. I learned eventually that anger was probably not the most appropriate reaction to such people. True, their behavior was purposeful and potentially hurtful, but the motivation behind their behavior was something completely different. People are often uncomfortable with things that do not match the way they think the world should be. It's almost without thought that they try to correct in some way—"He's not a *real* black man. He's an Uncle Tom."—their encounter with something outside the range

---

Scene: ANY CITY, USA

Black Delayer: What you waitin' on, homie?

Black Advancer (taken aback by Ebonics persistence and searching for explanation): I'm waiting for my wife to return. How about you, sir?

Black Delayer (taken aback by lack of Ebonics and searching for explanation): I'm waitin' on my squeeze too. You ain't from 'round here the way, huh?

Black Advancer: No. I'm from Chicago. I've only been here for a few months. However, this is quite an interesting city. Not as cosmopolitan as Chicago, but beginning to urbanize.

Black Delayer (monolingual skills being pressed to limit): Yeah. Where you cribbing?

Black Advancer (bilingual skills now in full force): In the Heights. It's a nice area.

Black Delayer: The Heights! You bullshitting? You a athlete or something?!

Black Advancer: No.

Black Delayer: Lottery?

Black Advancer: No.

Black Delayer: Pimp?

Black Advancer: No. I'm an accountant. What do you do?

Black Delayer: I work out at TWM. Second assistant crew chief. You know anybody need a gig? Cause I'm the man. I runs that bad boy.

Black Advancer: Good for you. I have to go. My wifey's waiting on me.

---

of what they are accustomed to. And by making this correction they can maintain the way they see the world. Accommodation and integration of new information can be very difficult for such people. (Remember Billy?)

Let's look at an example. You are walking down a busy city street and ahead you see a homeless person pushing a shopping cart. You know he is homeless because the cart is filled with an array of unrelated objects and a scrawny dog is walking along with him, tied to the cart. As you get closer you notice the clothes the homeless person is wearing are darkened by overuse and dirt. His face is filthy, and long, dirty hair covers his head. The nearer you come, the more pungent the man's odor becomes, and people in front of you are either crossing the street or giving the homeless person a wide berth. As you are about to pass, he looks up from his cart and says to you in the King's English, "Good Day. Sorry to trouble you. It seems that I have lost my way. If it wouldn't be too much of a bother would you please direct me to the nearest constable?"

For most of us the reaction would be shock. We are taken aback by a situation that probably matches nothing in our repertoire of experiences. After the initial shock, we find ourselves trying to make sense of it. We begin listing the possibilities:

"He must be an actor practicing for some part."

"Maybe, this is some kind of experiment being done to get people's reactions."

"Somebody's trying to pull a joke on me."

"It must be one of those reality TV shows. Where's the camera?"

We try to make sense of it. We attempt to somehow make this situation fit. Our brain almost hurts as we search for the proper place for this occurrence. You might protest that this example is unfair—that it doesn't count because it is an extreme example. But what is extreme is relative. For you, coming upon the unwashed, filthy English gentleman may be extreme. For another person, coming upon a well-educated and well-spoken black professional may be extreme. It all depends on exposure.

The social differential between us and the homeless person suddenly disappeared. We found ourselves scrambling for explanations for the ill-fitting circumstance. Not only does the change in social differential have consequences for our cognitive processing, there are significant self-esteem consequences for changes in social differentials. We may have thought ourselves better, smarter, more industrious than the homeless person. Now, we're not so sure.

Many black advancers find themselves in the position of the unwashed, filthy English gentleman. It is not unusual to deal with people who are trying to pigeonhole us. Most of us have had these encounters daily. Sometimes they are maddening because it seems that no matter how much we work, or how educated we are, there still remains this prejudice. There still remain these attempts to include us in a restricted scheme for all persons of our color.

However, the issue is only partly the person walking down the street. We advancers must be careful not to give such persons the power to affect our lives. We can become angry and frustrated. That's one way of dealing with such persons. And who wouldn't get angry? After all that work and sacrifice to reach our stations in life, we still are being questioned or scrutinized by some clown on the street. But when it really comes down to it, who cares what the clown on the street thinks or believes? We need not attend to satisfying such persons. Trying to convince them to change their worldview can only delay us in our own goals. And they may *never* be satisfied.

People who maintain stereotypic beliefs and attitudes remain very resistant to change. Even when faced directly with data that serves to disconfirm how they view the world, they simply weigh it less than data that confirms how they view the world.

How confirming and disconfirming data may be employed to protect one's worldview and sense of self is almost Machiavellian. In a subconscious fashion, confirming and disconfirming data may be used differentially and with such deft effectiveness that even the strong willed and self-aware might be seduced by their power. Ready-made schema and their hurtful, delimiting consequences emanate from many corners of humanity. We black Americans—particularly males—are accustomed to being perceived as "the bottom rung." Newly arriving immigrants, generations of racist Americans, and even unexposed foreigners manifest this scheme. Now do black delayers, in the face of unbridled upward movement by black advancers, join the usurpers? Do they too deny us our climb?

Chapter 15

APPLES AND ORANGES
Under the Skin and Over the Hump

They spend their time mostly looking forward to the past.
—John Osborne

La plus grande chose du monde, c'est de savoir etre a soi.
The greatest thing in the world is to know how to be oneself.
—Montaigne (Michel Eyquem de Montaigne)

I am always amazed how people who share melanin with me assume commonality with me. Somehow, for them, our closeness of hue translates to kinship of some sort. *Amazed* is the word I use because apparently that assumption of commonality and kinship fails to extend beyond what is processed through the ocular nerve. This must surely be the case, for what they see through their eyes fails to translate to their minds or hearts. Otherwise, how could they possibly visit such violence and mayhem upon their supposed kin? It is very possible that I am not sophisticated or smart enough to really understand the nuances involved in their thinking. Perhaps someone will someday enlighten me to what I seem to keep missing. But until such time, I will condemn their victimization of their "assumed" kin. Perhaps it's due to easy accessibility of victims. (After all, they're right there in front of them, all over the landscape). Or perhaps black criminals, like their victims, are having difficulty

> Scene: DR. DAVISON, ENTERING A PRISON
> FOR THE FIRST TIME
>
> Inmate: What's up, bro?
> Dr. Davison (smiling supportively): How are you?
> Inmate: I'm all right. You gonna be working here?
> Dr. Davison: Maybe. I'm just on a tour for right now.
> Inmate: We need you real bad here. All kind of scandalous shit
>   goes on 'round this camp.
> Dr. Davison (choosing not to bite): Well, if I get hired hopefully I'll
>   see you again. Take care.
> Inmate: All right, bro.

leaving the 'hood. It's curious because they could always take a bus back across town after a day of crime to return to the warm bosom of the 'hood. It all seems curious to me.

Similarity of skin color must constitute some significant meaning to them. I find it even more curious because they didn't let that similarity of skin color preclude them from abusing, robbing, beating down, raping, or murdering other black persons. For example, although black Americans represent only 12 percent of the US population, 45 percent of all victims of murder are black. Of those, 91 percent were killed by black Americans.[1]

Given the statistics related to black-on-black crime, it is not presumptuous for me to assume that the crime victims for these incarcerated persons were also black. Without a hint of logic, they have come to believe that we have things in common. However, it is likely I have more in common with my similarly trained and goal-directed white tour companions than I do with some black corner boy in search of a hustle or a tit to care for him. Now you can say that I'm in denial, but it's terribly true. Melanin is not connection. Similarity of goals, aspirations, history, reinforcement, and the like is connection. They are bums. I am not.

Their overutilization of the significance of melanin constitutes a *funda-*

mental racial error that serves to restrain and capture us all by misuse and mis-application of the characteristic of race. It is fundamental because it is erroneous in both directions—that is, just as it is wrong when propagated by white persons bent on circumscribing our activities, goals, aspirations, and futures, it is also wrong when foisted by black people bent on maintaining and perpetuating a false sense of connectedness and family. Moreover, if it is indeed the case that I have more in common with others who don't look like me, then I am pressed to follow suit, so to speak. That is, I will not rob, steal, and otherwise hurt people. I will be what I am: a psychologist. I will, and I must, evidence behaviors beyond the comforts of race. And, conversely, if I have more in common with those who look like me, then I am similarly pressed to follow suit. I must evidence behaviors that exist well within the comforts of race. To wit: I will hang with the homies.

For black advancers, with the importance of their forebears in mind, the choice is obvious.

Chapter 16

BLACK ADVANCERS
Conservatives, Uncle Toms, or Harbingers

We must dare to think "unthinkable" thoughts. We must learn to explore all the options and possibilities that confront us in a complex and rapidly changing world. We must learn to welcome and not to fear the voices of dissent. We must dare to think about "unthinkable things," because when things become unthinkable, thinking stops and action becomes mindless.

—James William Fulbright

Men can starve from a lack of self-realization as much as they can from a lack of bread.

—Richard Wright

Like most Americans of my era, I was schooled in the fundamental differences between people. I learned that black and white, rich and poor, uneducated and educated were different. I was taught that certain groups were at opposite ends of the human spectrum: that the chasm between those people should not—and in most cases could not—be spanned. Their differences were, by nature, unbridgeable. They were "them," and we were "us." Black was black and white was white; rich was rich and poor was poor. There was little rationale in trying to fight it. That's just the way it was.

But a profoundly strange and curious occurrence fell to me following the publication of my first book, *Prisoners of Our Past*. After each interview or appearance, I noticed an interesting commonality of opinion among persons presumed to be so very fundamentally different. From groups as disparate as the uneducated and educated, the rich and poor, the black and white, there arose a din whose consensus was staggering. From all poles, from all corners of humanity, people took exception to the invoking of black persons to take control of their lives and destinies—to wit, *to pull themselves up by the bootstraps.* In the opinions of these supposed "human opposites," I had, with little consideration for disturbing the natural order of things, wantonly attacked one of our country's most cherished myths: *Due to the injustices of the past, black people could not, and should not, be held responsible for their outcomes today.*

To my surprise, I had galvanized, in rather easy fashion, disparate groups of people. And for my attack upon this myth, I was indicted by all for *black conservatism*—so culturally repugnant and heinous a crime that no other words were deemed necessary. I was branded a being of low character—a rogue—a thief in the night. And what was my booty? It was the rationalizations and excuses employed by most Americans when discussing racial inequities.

Prisoners of Our Past was censored in several black bookstores. My writings were effectively dismissed and relegated to a pile of intellectual refuse. The epithet *black conservative* was rained down upon me as stones upon some Puritan-age witch. What evil magic and incantations would spew from such a being if not ostracized forthwith? After all, I had already recklessly asserted:

> The system provides the chains, but only we as individuals can clamp them shut.
> Black people should be held responsible for their own lives.
> We should stop blaming the white man for our problems.

Such disregard for our cherished myths had to be stopped.
The parade had to go on.

STRIKING UP THE BAND

Outspoken conservatism among black people seems to cause feelings of discomfort for all types of groups. But for black people in particular, merely noting "feelings of discomfort" is a gross understatement. Acrimony, accusations of cultural blasphemy, and malice are the reactions that await so-called black conservatives. We are bothered by words that do not fit the face. The black conservative is likened to a wayward family member. His or her pronouncements fly in the face of our family—a family, I might add, that is related neither by blood nor marriage, but by plain and unadorned melanin. Black conservatives—at least those brave enough to speak out—put us on Front Street, stripping and laying bare the ego defenses of a people already traumatized by American history. We become angered by their effrontery, their audacity. According to my own detractors, I had sold out, had forgotten from where I came, and desired to be white. You see, black persons are allowed an incredibly restricted latitude of opinion regarding racial matters, particularly if they want to be perceived as *black in good standing*. Individuality be damned: Lest we suffer public and private censure, all black persons have to adhere to a preapproved party line. For me, the choices were clear. I could exercise my individuality and incur social—and possibly physical—threats, or I could keep in step with popular black thought and not risk censure from the black community.

Fortunately, I found that my views were not as rabid as my detractors would have had me believe. For the last thirty years, our nation has been dealing increasingly with conservatism among black persons. Seminal writings by Thomas Sowell and Shelby Steele have given voice to legions of black persons previously disinclined to speak out against a sea of admonishment. To the chagrin of liberals and traditionalists alike, a significant and vocal conservatism has risen among black persons. But why does the rising of conservative black voices cause people to suspend—at least temporarily—their "fundamental" differences? What motivates them collectively to put aside their differences in order to admonish the heretic?

The answer lies in our expectations of the world. For most of us the notion of conservatism among black Americans runs counter to our cultural expectations. We expect black persons to identify strongly with the civil rights era—a period that helped to define a template for black ideas and behaviors. Then, on a daily basis, equal rights became part of the individual and collective consciousness of black Americans. Then we needed to band together for economic and political strength. But today the issue of civil rights no longer commands the full attention of the black community. Today we are faced with a great many possibilities for success and failure. And although economic and social opportunities are increasing, still many of us expect congruence between *black* struggles today and *black* struggles yesterday. For some of us, the long history of oppression and abuse has not been easy to forget or forgive. For those of us steeped in the rhetoric of that era, it has been difficult to let go of the past and lay claim to the future, particularly when that future is so very disparate from the experiences of our parents and grandparents.

For those of us who are more progressive, the prospect of improving our social and economic lot cannot be passed by. Future-minded individuals move deliberately toward success and improvement. Understandably, at the same time they distance themselves from those who simply want to recount history. The historic split forged between those who identify with the past and those who identify with the future remains, for black people, as deep and divisive today as it has ever been. It is *this* split that divides us so profoundly. Not conservatism, amount of black pride, or even economic stature. It is our orientation: that is, our facedness—backward or forward—that determines our outlooks, our associations, and ultimately our destinies.

Simply put, delayers choose to identify with the past. They characteristically hang onto the familiarity of the system's injustices. Delayers attribute success for any black person to luck, serendipity, or ingratiating behavior. But, more damaging, they unknowingly associate blackness with failure or interminable struggles. Staying *black*, being *brothers* and *sisters*, and *keeping it real* becomes an exercise in balancing aspirations and ethnic identity. Delayers, even those yet to be born, believe that "the system" is stacked mightily and indefatigably against all black persons.

In contrast, advancers choose to identify with the future. By and large these individuals embrace the American Dream of hard work and success.

They consider not only completing high school, but earning undergraduate and graduate degrees. Advancers look to the future for identity. They teach their children of the injustices of the system, but they also enjoin them to move beyond historic restraints and to not succumb to the history of oppression. Such persons are eager and willing to invest in the future. They attribute black success to ability and effort. And they succeed!

Those persons labeled today as black conservatives are related to advancers. They believe successes and failures are the result of effort and ability, not luck or ingratiating behavior. They believe that competition within the system will reap rewards. And for their beliefs they are—as was I—maliciously maligned by both black and white persons. Maligned for looking not to the past, but to the future. Maligned for questioning the inability or unwillingness of their brethren of color to take advantage of opportunities. But conservatives and advancers are not the same. Although similar in orientation toward the future, black conservatives and advancers differ significantly in their perspective regarding the system. Conservatives attempt to hold the system blameless for the conditions and obstacles faced by many black Americans. They contend that only laziness and motivation stand between black people and productive, successful lives. Black advancers, on the other hand, are like delayers regarding the system. They too hold the system responsible. However, unlike delayers, black advancers still choose to advance, irrespective of responsibility and blame.

Delayers fear that the successes black persons experience in the "white world" exact a significant price. They believe that black conservatives and black advancers have forgotten from where they came, severed connection to their roots, and lost sight of their blackness. I would argue that, ironically, it is these delayers who have forgotten not only from where they came—but also to where they are supposed to be going. Pathetically, it is *they* who have forgotten that people sacrificed and died so black persons might do a bit better, sacrificed and died so black persons might have an opportunity—an opportunity, *not* a guarantee. But, rather than building on the foundation set for them, delayers argue and lament past injustices and present-day difficulties. What cowards! Given that level of resolve, our forebears would never have dreamed of freedom, learned to read, attended college, or otherwise aspired to be more than just victims.

THE MARCH

For many delayers, looking at the world through a rearview perspective has become an art form, if not an inalienable right. *Slavery! Racism! Prejudice! Discrimination!* are sounded like battle cries, rallying the spirit and raising the ire of otherwise rational and reasonable persons. Such individuals seem compromised by some strange delirium that affects not only their volition to move forward, but their ability to respond rationally as well. While changing opportunities pass them by, black delayers march deliriously backward, banners of racial resistance held high.

Delayers cry foul at the suggestion that personal responsibility be a consideration in their probabilities of success. Suggestions such as these coming from white persons are tantamount to racism, they say. But white persons can be ignored or branded as racists. However, such statements from other black persons—particularly black conservatives and advancers—are not as easily dismissed. These brothers and sisters cannot be ignored. They usually command the attention of white persons and a media that may similarly and secretly have the same "conservative" beliefs.

Black conservatives and advancers represent challenges to our presumptions about racial identity. They have, for the most part, made it. They are successful economically and in their careers. They have gained access to spheres of interaction once strongly coveted and thought inaccessible by black persons. Ironically, it is the success of black conservatives and advancers that is so very unsettling to delayers! In a fashion, their successes highlight the failures of others. Moreover, their successes make rationalizations untenable. Delayers are left with little recourse but to proffer lamely that black conservatives and advancers have been lucky or sold out. To conclude otherwise is suicide—psychologically and politically—for those who have invested their careers, philosophies, and fragile egos in the past.

Struggling and achieving with little looking back, black advancers urge their brethren of color to join them in their advances. They encourage their peers to reject patterns that black communities and others have deemed appropriate for them. Black advancers demand to be treated as human and equals to all—not out of pity or because their forebears were enslaved, but in light of their individual strength and personal resolve. Rarely retreating, black advancers push forward, accepting personal responsibility for their outcomes. Unfortunately, for those black persons who dare to espouse a philosophy of personal responsibility, many critics reserve the terribly inaccurate term *black conservative*. Only our recently acquired political correctness checks us from using the more derogatory term *Uncle Tom*. But whether Uncle Tom or black conservative, the term still denotes, in many minds, a traitor of sorts. Traitorous to exactly what, no one seems to know. In my slightly biased opinion, if any group should be considered traitorous, it is the delayers! They choose to wait, to blame, and to look backward rather than building on the foundation set for them by their forebears. Delayers have reneged on the souls and sacrifices of their ancestors. It is they who have been traitorous to The Struggle. It is they who have extinguished the fire.

I daresay that in many eyes, any black person who has not embraced the victimization philosophy—so popular today in American culture—is considered a black conservative. Black conservatives, in the minds of many, are not representative or "authentic" black persons. Their very existence taxes our psyches. Their viability challenges us to increase the range of black values, goals, aspirations, and desires. They demonstrate, every day, that success and respect is attainable in America for everyone—not just for white males or the children of the affluent, but for everyone. For those contributions alone, black conservatives and black advancers should be applauded, not censured. That we applaud delayers and censure conservatives speaks greatly to the identity of black people and with whom we will align our interests and futures.

YOU CAN'T FOOL ALL OF THE PEOPLE
ALL OF THE TIME

But me? A conservative? The thought of so dastardly a possibility clanged dissonantly with my self-concept. I had never imagined that achievement and effort would be viewed as anything but positive. Especially when that achievement and effort comes from a member of a group that has been historically disenfranchised. The label *black conservative* was bothersome to me. I considered that there must be some reprieve from so unjust an appellation. But where to turn? My detractors had amply demonstrated their irrationality. Turning to them would prove futile. And too many of my supporters had become uncharacteristically mute in response to the prospect of conflict with the mass of delayers represented in black communities.

In search of some relief from this injustice, and with just a hint of desperation, I flipped through my trusty *Webster's Third New International Dictionary*. (I have long considered reference books a key to rational and good living.) Hoping—searching—I turned the pages, and then I found it. My salvation. Under the word *conservative*: "of or relating to a political party, point of view, or philosophy that advocates preservation of the established order and views proposals for change critically and usu[ally] with distrust." I paused, absorbing the words. What? Could it be? This definition sounded more akin to many of my detractors, who refused to stray from their antiquated methods and ideas. They refused to consider any thought or conversation without a cognitive template of the 1950s and 1960s. It was *they* who maintained existing views of race relations while asserting the improbability of success. It was *they* who interacted with others in stereotypic, habitual ways—never changing strategies or outlooks. It was *they* who seemed to relish unchanging conditions so they could continue to fuel their fires of rationalization and oppression.

I smirked at the revelation. They had caused me to think myself out of step—that it was *I* who wasn't hip to what was happening, that it was *I* who was conservative. These delayers had duped me—and an awful lot of other folk. My behaviors and ideas had been anything but conservative. Trying to improve one's social and economic lot by rejecting traditional societal and black community standards for achievement seemed antithetical to conservative. Piqued by this antithesis, I reached for my thesaurus—fully confident that my detractors and antagonists were lacking such resources in their libraries. I turned its pages and I found *conservative*. Listed as a contrast was the word *progressive*. Back to my dictionary I clamored, spilling along the way a copy of Joseph Campbell's *The Power of Myth*. I found it—*progressive*: "of, relating to, or characterized by progress: devoted to or evincing continuous improvement: making use of or interested in new ideas, inventions, or opportunities."

Well, well, well. Again my trusty dictionary had provided rescue from the clutches of ignorance. But ignorance is not the whole issue when addressing delaying concerns. Also at issue is the desperate clinging to the past that is so characteristic of delayers. Irrespective of its utility in their personal lives, delayers live in the past. They lament its effects on their present and future. Desperate for an ever-present audience, they encourage others to remember our genesis and heritage. However, the implication that black advancers deny or forget their genesis is erroneous. Advancers are as painfully aware of the past as are delayers. Advancers just choose not to orient to the past, but rather to the present and future.

This difference in orientation accounts for both a rift among black people and confusion for the rest of America. Fortunately, that rift and confusion is good for us all! It makes arriving at some unifying theme of *black* consciousness difficult—a theme that would, in essence, chain us all together. As a nation, we are looking for, hoping for, and acclimated to a single, invariant, and predictable black perspective. That has been the case historically, and, sadly, still seems the case in many minds. Why else would we assume that those black persons who deviate from popular black opinion are somehow less black or are Uncle Toms? Why else would we dismiss them summarily and cast aspersions upon their *black* character? But now, more than ever, varied black perspectives have to be respected and embraced. Otherwise we will continue to alienate large segments of our population. Worse, we will continue to alienate ourselves from our respective destinies.

Still, many people—including ourselves—are bothered by our variance.

None of us seems to know from year to year or from day to day what our world-view should be. We cannot even agree whether to be Afro-Americans, African Americans, brothers and sisters, blacks, niggers, or just Americans. So many profound questions of identity remain. Are we still the disenfranchised group traditionally striving for equality and respect in this nation, or are we the successful, entrepreneurial persons sometimes portrayed on television and in magazines? Are we moving forward, onward, and upward; or are we stuck in an ennobled rut of rationalization? Have we rejected being included in the life stream of US society and moved toward separatism, or have we overcome them *and* ourselves?

The answer to each of these questions is *yes*. We are *all* these things: separatists, merchants, successes, failures, poor, rich, stuck, advancing, optimistic, and vanquished. Despite the efforts of our leaders and benefactors to level our differences, we continue to expand beyond the historic limitations set for us. The range of what is *black* continues to be expanded. But with that expansion must come acceptance of the advancers and their vision. This, in my opinion, is one of our most pressing issues toward psychological freedom, mental health, and respect in US society. Otherwise, as long as people—particularly us—treat the values, ideas, and behaviors of black people as monolithic, we will receive little respect as *individuals* free to conform, dissent, succeed, or fail. Tragically, those of us who don't fit the norm of what is *black* will continue to be ostracized.

STOPPING THE PARADE

Many of our strangely anointed leaders rant that they know what is good for us, that they know what we all need. Moreover, they imply that until all black persons—each and every one of us—are economically solvent, America has not lived up to its creed. Our leaders (and their delaying followers) claim that America has a debt to pay to these descendants of slaves, that the potentiality for success for each and every black person has somehow been compromised by a history of unequal treatment. They imply that we are owed reparations to give us equal footing on the ladder to success. This is utter nonsense. There will always be some persons who are successful and some who are unsuccessful in a competitive economic environment. And, as such, there will always be some persons—black, white, and otherwise—who don't "make it" economically. To hold the nation a psychological and moral hostage for the inability or unwillingness of some to achieve is indefensible. We need to accept that some black people will not make it—not now or ever. *Accept it!*

Rather than wrestling with the unattainable goal of empowerment and success for all, what needs to be determined is an acceptable and equitable level of poverty for black Americans. It is a given that some proportion of our nation will be impoverished. The goal is now to arrive at a reasonable and equitable impoverishment rate across all groups. Is it 2 percent, 5 percent, 15 percent of all black persons? Perhaps we need to press economists for the figure—to arrive at such a figure would be almost therapeutic for us and the entire nation. Instead of a battle toward the nebulous goal of economic equality, we would have a determinable target. The acceptance of such a numerical and cognitive precept would free us from the bonds of racial parity. As well, we could free ourselves from the interminable battle for "equality." We could break ranks and live our lives unencumbered by the unwieldy swords and armor of the black struggle. Our struggles would be our own. We could no longer hold "them" and their descendants eternally responsible for our well-being. We would have to relinquish our tenacious hold of past injustices and wrongs and concentrate on the present and the future. Moreover, we would be responsible individually for our own livelihoods, our own happiness, and our own success and failure.

Granted, we would lose some of our collectivity—a collectivity that is at times stifling. We would still be black, but without feeling yoked to a history of oppression or each other. The historic sharedness of racial oppression would be passé as each individual would be responsible for her lot. Individually, we would be judged by our successes and failures. We would lose the safety of numbers—something black Advancers have been forever doing without. Only the power of our own individual motivations and the strength of our own individual efforts would define how well we do. As well, the self-defeatist behavior of other black persons would have no race-specific consequence for us as individuals. We would learn to cherish our own individuality while respecting the individualities of others—even that of supposed Uncle Toms, black conservatives, and black advancers. We would no longer be yoked by race. We would be free to be, to think, and to aspire toward what we want without having to do so in black. Oh, how therapeutic! It would be like one gigantic group therapy.

Such pronouncements are not as unfamiliar and divergent as they sound. Other Uncle Toms, black conservatives, and black advancers in US history have exhorted us to judge and be judged by our personal motivations and skills. One of those Uncle Toms, in particular, encouraged us to be judged "not by the color of our skin, but by the content of our character." That's right! One of those Toms was Martin Luther King Jr. And if we black people are truly honest with ourselves and remember accurately back to those days, Martin also had to deal with being perceived as an Uncle Tom and black conservative. Oh, you can deny it if you want. But it's true—painfully true. And you know it! The canonizing of dead leaders and their resulting greatness often clouds our memories of their humanness as well as our initial reaction to them. But, without a doubt, there were significant portions of the black community that branded Martin Luther King Jr. an Uncle Tom or a black conservative. That was before he gained deity status. Remember?

And, while we're on the subject, another Uncle Tom asked us to consider the humanness of all people, to consider that black, white, and all others needed to work communally toward dignity and respect. Sure, he may have started out with a very exclusionist tone, separating the victimized black population from the "blue-eyed devils." But after seeing the light, so to speak, he came to believe in the brotherhood of humankind and how all of our destinies are intertwined. That's right! It was Malcolm X who, after some growth and maturation, suggested such a philosophy. But we all know what he got for his trouble.

Whenever change is suggested or whenever people are asked to look in the mirror, resistance will follow. This is true for individuals, couples, families, large groups, and societies. So whenever someone black suggests a change from the philosophies and strategies of the hallowed great civil rights era, there will be resistance. Whenever someone black suggests there is perhaps a cooperative, nonrhetorical, and humanistic way to address racial concerns, he will bring down upon himself the brands Uncle Tom, traitor to the race, and black conservative. But I consider myself in good company.

Whether labeled black conservatives or black advancers, they are grossly misrepresented as traitorous to the race. Black advancers are, in actuality, *progressives* looking intently toward the future and employing a variety of strategies toward success. By adapting and expanding to changing conditions, they challenge the status quo regarding how black persons are perceived. They are, in essence, progressive in their outlook and response to changing social and economic conditions for our nation.

All persons who remain tied to a philosophy that hoists victimization and delaying perspectives as banners are likely doing more harm to their race peers than any Uncle Tom, black conservative, or even white supremacist could possibly ever hope to do. Black delayers, perhaps unknowingly, maintain the status quo by refusing to depart from the same invariant strategy for the advancement of black people. Delayers do not expand or adapt to changing conditions. They keep themselves, their children, their brethren, and even their possible white allies firmly cemented in the past. The future is in front of them and they shy away from it. Instead, they look toward the past. They become lost in their rhetoric, and they want others to join them in their morass. They are, in essence, *conservative* in their approach to the problems of race in this country. I cannot join them.

Besides, I hate parades.

They have forgotten the struggle . . . and they have forgotten the road over which we have come, and they are not teaching it to their children.
    —ALEX HALEY

NOTES

CHAPTER 4: GHETTO FABLES: AESOP AIN'T GOT NOTHING ON US

1. This split in black consciousness probably also existed during the three-hundred-year enslavement period. However, during that period, few opportunities, save escape, were available for its enactment and expression.

2. *Cultural schizophrenia* refers to the existence of multiple and simultaneous identities. Such existence, while normative for any group comprised of millions of individuals, seems to pose problems as people seek to maintain a singularity and unity of being for black Americans.

CHAPTER 5: WHY BIG MOMMA'S FEETS HURT SO MUCH

1. Interestingly, there exists no enduring analogous place for the black patriarch. "Big Daddy" and "Big Poppa," although sometimes used in a familial context, more often refer to men who move in pimp and player circles. The Big Daddy type was known to exist in affluent white families and referred to the man who owned and ran his family like he owned and ran the local factory.

CHAPTER 9: IT'S ALL YOUR FAULT: NAH, NAH, NAH, NAH, NAH, NAH

1. The forgetting of history and being therefore destined to repeat its mistakes is common among people. However, for persons still grappling to reach an equal footing economically, socially, and psychologically, lapses in memory are tantamount to journeying without compass, sextant, or map.

CHAPTER 10: BAA, BAA, BLACK SHEEP: BLACK LEADERS AND THEIR WINDMILLS

1. US Census Bureau, March 2001 Current Population Survey.

2. Increasing change in this practice has become evident. In relatively recent history, a proliferation of churches that minister specifically to the black middle class has occurred. The advent of these institutions speaks volumes about the evolving stature of black Americans.

3. Despite its lack of place for them, many middle-class black persons remain, nonetheless, intimidated enough to attend traditional black churches. Some, largely motivated by years of attending as children, unthinkingly continue their association. Others are likely slumming: using traditional church like a trip to the 'hood to get ribs or chicken, keeping connected and keeping it real.

CHAPTER 12: TICKETS TO THE NEW MINSTREL SHOWS

1. Lest I be criticized for being inaccurate, let's define *minstrel show*. I would say it is a stereotypic—sometimes comedic—depiction of black culture and people, usually performed by white actors in blackface. Think critically about the last black-oriented play, film, music video, or girlfriend novel you partook of. Need I say more? I rest my case.

2. One might argue that if a person were, let's say, Lithuanian American, his culture would play a part in who he is—assuming his parents kept cultural traditions alive. However, the keeping alive of some black traditions (e.g., maintaining adver-

sarial relationship to the "white" world, remaining overly enmeshed) keeps us dead in the water while the rest of the world sails by.

CHAPTER 13: THERE BUT FOR THE GRACE OF GOD GO I (AND OTHER LUNACY)

1. Moreover, such statements serve as testament to the lack of efficacy and self-determination historically assumed for all black Americans.

CHAPTER 15: APPLES AND ORANGES: UNDER THE SKIN AND OVER THE HUMP

1. Statistics computed by the Center for Healing Hearts and Spirits, which is a project of the Women's Council on African-American Affairs, Inc.

SUGGESTED READING

Bennett, Lerone. *Before the Mayflower: A History of Black America*. Chicago: Johnson Publishing, 2003.

Blair, Thomas Lucien Vincent. *Retreat to the Ghetto: The End of a Dream?* New York: Hill and Wang, 1977.

Du Bois, William Edward Burghardt. *The Souls of Black Folk*. New York: Barnes & Noble Classics, 1903.

Franklin, John Hope. *An Illustrated History of Black Americans*. New York: Time-Life Books, 1973.

Lott, Eric. *Love and Theft: Blackface Minstrelsy and the American Working Class*. New York: Oxford University Press, 1993.

Shelby, Tommie. *We Who Are Dark: The Philosophical Foundations of Black Solidarity*. Cambridge, MA: Belknap Press of Harvard University Press, 2005.

Sowell, Thomas. *Race and Culture: A World View*. New York: Basic Books, 1994.

Steele, Shelby. *A Dream Deferred: The Second Betrayal of Black Freedom in America*. New York: HarperCollins, 1999.

Tarpley, Natasha. *Testimony: Young African-Americans on Self-Discovery and Black Identity*. Boston: Beacon Press, 1994.

White, John. *Black Leadership in America*. New York: Longman, 1990.

Part 3

MESSAGES FOR THOSE MOVING FORWARD

Part 3 addresses identity beyond the mantle of race. Having rid our-selves of the burden of those who choose to delay, we now turn to exploring life without the limitations of race. Identity beyond the struggle and overcoming ourselves constitutes much of the writing in this section. Discussion of how we have been duped into giving back to the wrong community is offered. Suggestions are given for dealing with feelings of uncertainty, marginality, jealousy, and anger. A theory of fearlessness is offered to help explore emancipation of self and becoming the new you. Finally, nurturance and development of self beyond race is offered as the vehicle through which psychological freedom is achieved.

Chapter 17

YOU CAN'T DANCE YOUR WAY OUT OF YOUR CONSTRICTIONS

Procrastination is opportunity's assassin.
—VICTOR KIAM

Eighty percent of success is showing up.
—WOODY ALLEN

First, my apologies to George Clinton and the Funkadelics. Their seminal work was a hit when I was a young adult. The jam was bad. I loved that music. Who could top "Do you promise to funk, the whole funk, nothin' but the funk?" Back in the day we danced, smoked, drank, and tore the roof off. We partied hard, but not into oblivion. I'm afraid many of those being left behind due to their delay are doing just that: partying into oblivion.

Historically and culturally, celebration for black Americans has been a deeply ingrained tradition. From enslavement through Jim Crow to the present, celebration has been employed as a means of bonding for black communities and strengthening of resiliency for black individuals. Historically, doors of opportunity were sealed shut, bolted from the other side, and guarded by sentries. In the face of such obstacles, celebration lifted our spirits, bolstered our resolve, and girded us for next week's rejections. However, for today's black Americans as a group, many of our difficult times have passed. We have suc-

---

Scene: SISTER THELMA RETURNING FROM COLLEGE,
GRADUATED AND READY

Donnetta: Girl, I ain't seen you in a long-ass time. Where you
been?

Thelma: Working days and going to school at night. It took me
five years, but I got my RN. I finally got it.

Donnetta: Damn, girl. I ain't know you was still in school.

Thelma: Yeah, I was. Dee, you're smart. Why don't you go
down there? They're always looking for good students and
you was always good with the books. Better than me!

Donnetta: Girl, you trippin'. I'm thirty-five. I can't be going down
there with them kids. I'm too old. What'd you say it took you?
Five years? Shit, I'll be almost forty.

Thelma: You're gonna be forty in five years anyway, Dee. You
can be forty with a career or trade, or forty saying "I'll be
almost forty-five when I'm done."

---

cessfully pushed aside those oppressors who were set to deter and thwart us, and we have pushed doors wide open. Why does all the partying continue?

Partying and all other forms of avoidance serve as ego defense mechanisms—that is, if I stop partying/having constant sex/getting high/working on my jump shot/being a criminal, then I must assess my skills and qualifications, survey employment opportunities, and get out there to challenge others for jobs and careers. Otherwise, I am a bum—living off the efforts of others and disinterested in standing up as a viable adult in society. In the face of such reality, partying is much more palatable an endeavor than facing a mirror and finding oneself wanting.

A chosen lifestyle of living from one party to the next serves to mask one's lack of efficacy. It's a fraudulent attempt at adulthood. Children, work, and family are treated as fillers along the way between parties. Meanwhile, opportunities, time, and resources that could have effected movement forward and heralded attainment of adulthood are squandered—left in half-empty cans of beer and cannabis seeds spit out onto the floor. More important, attempting to dance your way out of your constriction instead of positively applying your skills represents resistance to leaving the 'hood—physically, emotionally, and psychologically. Why else would one spend so much precious time, money, and ego in pursuit of the most bomb party? It keeps us distracted from the realities of intergenerational accountability and responsibility—that is, we'll let other black persons—responsible and accountable black persons—forward the goals of upward mobility for our people. Your responsibility? Keep the party going!

In order to effect one's way out of the 'hood, one must begin to see dancing as insufficient. Knowing the latest step, handshake, or cool greeting must become irrelevant. We must get out of the 'hood physically, emotionally, and psychologically. There just is no manner of dancing, jiving, rapping, or cooling your way out of your constriction. Some of us will grow—spiritually, emotionally, and psychologically—beyond the ghetto. Others of us will not grow at all, because for them the most enduring and indelible ghetto is in their own minds.

In our minds are the street corners. In our minds are the lack of opportunities, the blocked paths, and the ever-thwarting white man. We must get out there—physically, emotionally, and psychologically out there—into the world outside the 'hood. We must let go of our comfort. Dancing your way out of your constriction is regressive and self-serving. Getting—and, for many, staying—high is regressive. It is not because you are black that the world is a ghetto. The world is a ghetto because *you make your world a ghetto!* I think such attitudes account for why so many of us failed to take advantage of opportunities in the 1970s. If you want to get out of the ghetto, then you must stop dancing. Register for classes and leave the stupid ones behind. Identify and pursue a career and leave the losers and their excuses behind. Make a commitment beyond learning the Electric Slide or Lean Wit It, Rock Wit It. Move toward a new and satisfying life and dump the anchors tied 'round your neck. Let it all go—all of it. And move on. Do it! Otherwise, you'll only dance your way into oblivion.

What's funny is that some of those people at the club dancing with you are only slumming. They have advanced into wonderful careers and lifestyles, and now come down to the 'hood every so often to dance with y'all, eat some chicken and ribs, and then return to their middle-class—or better—lives. I know it's true. I've done it myself. Y'all make good chicken and ribs, but terrible role models.

You have to want more. You have to identify it and pursue what you want relentlessly. Perhaps you can't go to nursing school full-time. Break it down. Take a course or two a semester. Before you know it, you'll be there. How long have you complained about lack of opportunity at some penny-ante job? A year? Two? Ten? Take a good hard look at yourself and the road you're on. Is it the one you want to be on? If not, get off it. You might find you are getting in your own way.

Stop saying that those middle-class black folks aren't "real" black people/ brothers and sisters/Gs/homies. Stop saying that they're not true to the game or down for the cause. They're just as real and true as you. In fact, they're probably more real and more true, because they're moving forward—as our forebears envisioned for us all. Those middle-class blacks are the true warriors of our communities. They fight the war. They saddle up every day and ride into the fray. Dancers and delayers are nothing more than stable hands, and poor ones at that. If you want to see real discrimination and prejudice, put yourself in a position to challenge institutional racism like middle-class blacks do every day. That's where it exists. Out there is where it lives. You don't see real discrimination and prejudice in the ghetto. It's not on the corner where you stand holding your crotch. It's not on the stoop or in the kitchen where you stand plaiting hair. No one's challenging you there. Stop pretending that they are. Your only challenge is living for the next chance to get high, for the next party, for the next piece of ass. *You* must take a chance. What have you got to lose other than lame excuses? You have much to gain. And what you gain will be spectacular.

Chapter 18

DENIAL IS MORE THAN
A RIVER IN AFRICA

This one makes a net, this one stands and wishes.
Would you like to make a bet which one gets the fishes?
    —CHINESE RHYME

Others may argue about whether the world ends with a bang or a whisper. I
just want to make sure mine doesn't end with a whine.
    —BARBARA GORDON

Generally, people are motivated to maintain a sense of efficacy for themselves, either through their achievements or through self-delusion. We want our egos stroked, not destroyed. We like to see ourselves as competent and valid. Denial is one of several defense mechanisms that may be easily employed to protect one's ego. By deflecting responsibility for one's circumstances, a person might avoid nagging doubts about ability, motivation, and drive. For example, by blaming discriminatory practices or institutional racism, an individual might protect himself from criticism of his chronically sporadic employment.

The denial defense mechanism is deeply engrained in the psyches of black delayers. As long as the white man is empowered psychologically as oppressor, black delayers are freed—in their minds—from negatively evaluating their

Scene: UP THE STREET FROM PETE'S BAR AND GRILL

Larry: Woman, I'm so tired of you sweating me 'bout some damned job. Day and night, night and day pressing me. That's all I hear from you.

Renee: Baby, you got to get something. We just ain't gonna be able to make it like this.

Larry: Girl, I'm a black man! Maybe you ain't realized it yet, but white people don't like hiring no brothers unless they ain't got no choice at all. That's just the way it is.

Renee: I know it's hard, but . . .

Larry (interrupting): Hard?! My Daddy damn near kilt his self trying to work for white people. Trying to please them. His knees and back's so hurt he barely ever gets out his chair. I ain't going out like that. Period!

Renee (fighting tears): Maybe if you got some training or something it might make it easier to find some kind of work. Even a piece of a job could help. Belinda's husband went to that trade school downtown, and now he's making good money.

Larry: Belinda's husband's an Uncle Tom. Walking 'round like he's better. He ain't nothing. Just another white black man. You want me like that?

own motivations, strengths, and egos. The argument goes this way: "It doesn't matter what I do, how much school I attend, or how hard I work. The white man has no place in his world for me." So instead of taking personal responsibility for one's circumstances—good or bad—one is constantly trying to rationalize nonparticipation in what is perceived as "the white man's world." At one point in history—and justifiably—black people demonized most white persons and the system that operated to enslave, oppress, and disenfranchise them. But now, pathetically, black delayers seek to invoke that same demonization toward the relatively innocent and distant descendants of those slavers. Their argument is increasingly weak and spurious. Moreover, the demon has been defanged and laid low by black advancers. It is resuscitated and empowered only through black delay and inaction.

Black delayers—unprepared for today's educational and motivational demands—are increasingly under attack from many quarters. People from ethnic and nonethnic groups attack them. People with conservative and liberal viewpoints attack them. Fifth-generation Americans and newly arriving immigrants attack them. All point skeptically at the unprepared. Even the parents and siblings of the chronically unprepared are beginning to question the initiative and ambition of these kinsmen. For these albatrosses, lack of preparedness has caused a crisis of monumental proportions. Previously these black men and women had been given sway due to the purported injustices of the system. Now their position as victim has become untenable. Simply citing prejudice, racism, discrimination, the legacy of slavery, or unjust system has become insufficient harbor. Increasingly, black delayers are seen as bums, lamely employing the rhetoric of injustice to shield themselves from accountability. Increasingly, they are running out of excuses, running out of ways to justify their lack of motivation. Given their dwindling retreats for ego protection, black advancers and others may fittingly ask, "Why are we at all tolerating their bullshit?"

Black delayers, your game has been peeped and I'm calling you out. I'm putting your raggedy ass on Front Street—putting you on blast. You have for too long hidden behind the cloak of race, far too long floated lazily down a river forged through sacrifice and death. You have far too long dragged upon our coattails. Far too long have you disrespected and done disservice to the efforts of our forebears. You are our worst enemies, our worst liabilities, our worst representatives. Your smug recalcitrance has become bothersome. You are bums, plain and simple. Get off your bum ass or get left behind. Bottom line!

We have achieved greatly in the scant 150 years since emancipation. No area of business, commerce, or politics remains unaffected by the significant contributions of black Americans. Only by burying one's head in the sand can anyone suggest that unprecedented achievements and opportunities have not been realized by black Americans. Yet there exist significant portions of our communities that do just that. Rather than taking responsibility for their sloth and lack of preparedness, they look outside themselves—attributing their failures and stage-of-life difficulties to the machinations of the white man. Black delayers much too easily accept the white man's omnipotence. Individual denial for black delayers becomes group activity as notes of self-delusion are compared on the street corners and in the taprooms of the 'hood. The resultant tales of blocked opportunities gain increasing "credibility" with each telling. Delayers then come to believe their own tales. That's delusion!

In order to move beyond denial, it is crucial to take stock of oneself (i.e., to look into the mirror). By doing so, individuals may free themselves from tired old rhetoric and move toward addressing those aspects of themselves that are in need of identification. That's growth! Words like

I'm weak.
I'm scared.
I need some support.
I might have to leave my spouse.
I'm lazy.

Scene: MOST CORNERS IN THE 'HOOD

Big Pimpin': I heard they hiring down at TWM, but when I went down there, they ain't have nothing. Whole lot of white people standing 'round looking at me. Man, ain't nothing down there dark 'cept night.

Sugar Bear: Yeah. Same thing happened to me when my woman made me go down there. They ain't 'bout to hire no brothers. Man asked me did I have a resume. Like I'm gonna spend good money on some shit like that. I said, "Hey man. Y'all got a gig or not?" Next thing I know, he had an emergency call to make.

Big Pimpin': They never hire nobody black down there.

Sugar Bear: I heard that!

DAVISON'S MANIFESTO

I hereby absolve all white persons of responsibility for the conditions of black Americans today. Individually and collectively, they are hereby released from the mantles of blame and guilt. From this day forward, they may proceed with their lives—unaffected by the ravings of black underachievers, black delayers, and their rabid agents. Intimidation and harassment will no longer be their penalty for the transgressions of generations past. No longer must they apologize for their whiteness.

You are hereby free to live your lives, raise your children, pursue your happiness, and attain your fullest potential. You need no longer serve as scapegoats for those who refuse to build on the efforts of their forebears. No longer should you feel shame at the squalor and degradation of poor blacks. They too are free to live their lives, raise their children, pursue their happiness, and attain their fullest potential. Let's hope these black American descendants of slaves will do so. After all, you can't stop us anymore. Only we can stop us.

I don't like myself as I am now.

Maybe it's not the white man; maybe it's me.

are scary, but they represent the first steps toward advancement and psychological freedom.

Chapter 19

ON BECOMING LACTOSE INTOLERANT

None of us are responsible for our birth. Our responsibility is the use we make of life.
—JOSHUA HENRY JONES

Failure can get to be a rather comfortable old friend.
—MIGNON MCLAUGHLIN

More than crack cocaine or cultures of criminality, the legion numbers of black men refusing to stand up and take responsibility for their children, their community, or even themselves likely represents the greatest calamity visited upon black America today. Their irresponsibility emanates largely from the perception that they represent the very bottom rung on the ladder of achievement. They are, therefore, by definition incapable of self-sufficiency or the care of others. Rather, they need to be cared for. Black men, black women, newly arriving immigrants, and society in general contribute greatly to this perception of black males as nigger to the world. What we all get out of maintaining this relationship is pure and simple ego enhancement.

Black delaying women, for example, often fail to put pressure upon black boys and men to stand up. They rear their boys often as psychological cripples,

189

unpressured by the vicissitudes that other groups must face. As regards active participation in our competitive society, the axiom "It's Hard on a Black Man Out There" is taught to boys and girls. This instilling of weakness in black boys to ensure that plenty will remain at the bottom rung for the rest of the world—even black women—to measure themselves against is tantamount to fratricide.

During a casual drive through any large US city, visitors will be astonished by legions of black men milling about—doing nothing and planning little else. Somehow they survive. Mothers take care of them. Girlfriends and wives take care of them. Even their sisters, grandmothers, and aunties take care of them. Petty criminality provides them sustenance. Living the street life and staying "true to the game" provides them peers of similar circumstance and delusion. And once their female resources are exhausted, incarceration provides them shelter from the slings and arrows of their critics.

I've worked several prisons during my career as a psychologist. The one thing that always strikes me is the ease with which black men acclimate to prison life. They don't often seem to be very bothered by their circumstances. Many interact with each other as if at a country club. Whether sharing stories, posturing for each other, or planning their next ruinous debacle, they seem acclimated and satisfied with their circumstances.

One could argue, romantically, that strength of mind and the warrior spirit sustains such men. Some have even likened these black men to political prisoners—victims of an ongoing war between the haves and the have-nots. But it is so much more than that. These black men seem to be enjoying prison. "Three hots and a cot" is often the retort heard when questioning their status. In essence, the root of their acclimation and comfort is the lack of pressure and lack of accountability that incarceration provides. In prison, no one is pressing them about child rearing, fathering, or husbanding obligations. Instead, they stand around "kickin' it"—laughing, holding their crotches, and telling lies about what they had on the streets.

These black men are, in fact, enabled. They are enabled by a community that refuses to hold them directly responsible for their part in caring for themselves and their families. They are enabled by mothers, girlfriends, wives, Big Mommas, and aunties who, concerned about "little Boo," make it easy for him to survive. If those enablers were absent, these black men would likely perish. After all, they have little education, few skills, and no prospects.

Black boys commonly hear from their delayer mothers, "You're just like your father"—thus setting up a self-fulfilling prophecy. "I'm just like my father: no good with zero prospects." That identity is soon fulfilled as young males seek out negative, but supportive, role models. Ultimately, a schism develops between black men and women, with the former choosing not to hear themselves ridiculed and maligned, and the latter in their minds gaining a toehold on the rung above black males. Emotional castration is the goal: castration at home, castration at school, castration in society. Many of these men feel the only places where they can function as men are in beds producing children, on the streets producing trouble, and in prison producing delusions.

WHAT? NO COOKIES?!

There exist many black men who need to become lactose intolerant—that is, much less dependent upon the tit of survival provided by Mom and girlfriend or society's jails and prisons. We need to step up and step out: "Ante up and kick in like men. Like men!" as stated in the film *Glory*. Yes, it is hard on a black man out there. Very hard. So what? What are your choices? Either ante up and become men or slither over to the trough. If it's the latter you choose, then you're cowardly punks. What we as black men have to deal with today is absolutely insignificant compared to what black men had to deal with fifty, seventy-five, or one hundred years ago. Nothing at all! Nobody's trying to lynch you. Nobody's trying to stop you from reading. Nobody's raping your wife, selling your children, or burning crosses on your lawn.

The indignities our black forebears faced in order to advance us to this juncture in time were incredible. They faced those indignities and they persevered. The only indignities of any consequence that I now face as a black man are those fueled by these sorry-ass brothers: Queued and chained as they enter prison. Approaching my car to sell crack cocaine. Too lazy to rise in the morning in order to wait in line for daily journeyman work. Sporting gold chains and teeth while their babies go without diapers. Impregnating young girls with no intention of caring for their offspring. These indignities I face every day as I set off for work, read the newspaper, or watch television reports of their latest bullshit.

Yes, the media is biased. Yes, *they* put crack in your neighborhood. So what?! Delayers behave as if they have no choice but to commit crimes, impregnate, and use or sell drugs. They do have choices. They're just too cowardly to exercise them. That's not my fault, the media's fault, or the drug lord's fault. That's their fault! Get off your butt, get off the tit, and do something. Now!

I encourage those of us who are more well heeled and well motivated to release these never-weaning brothers from our psyches. They impinge mightily upon our psychological freedom. We have duped ourselves into believing that these boys and men are victims in need of help and understanding. Through guilt for being successful, we have become tied into an interminable battle for opportunities for these increasingly distant relatives. We have become codependent in their self-perpetuating morass, enmeshed with their unaccountability. We hold fundraisers; they drink. We contribute time and money; they hustle. We lament their future; they reproduce and make application to prison.

I challenge this fraternity of failure. To their guild, I refuse to pledge.

Chapter 20

DUMPING POOKIE

He's Heavy and He Damned Sure Ain't My Brother

Nature never makes any blunders; when she makes a fool she means it.
—Josh Billings (Henry Wheeler Shaw)

Remember always that you have not only the right to be an individual, you have an obligation to be one.
—Eleanor Roosevelt

Pookie Wilson is my cousin. We grew up walking the same streets, drinking the same Kool-Aid, plotting on the same girls. Somewhere Pookie took a wrong turn. He's my cousin and I love him, but he's scandalous. Impregnating a girl nowhere near legal age, pawning his mother's wedding ring, creating a food stamps business scam, and snatching women's purses on the first of the month are just a few of my cousin's highlights.

It seems we all have Pookies in our lives. Often the family tolerates them, and the old people enjoin us to embrace Pookie and his maladaptive behaviors. "He's family," they remind us. But dumping persons from one's life who are encased by poverty or prison bound is probably the single most important accomplishment in your journey toward psychological freedom. Ridding ourselves of all our Pookies—mine, yours, and theirs—will aid us all in our advancement.

How do we not become embarrassed when they insist on embarrassing us? How do you become *you* while having to drag all of this dead weight with you? Letting go of dysfunction in black communities in general, as well as dysfunction in specific black persons toward whom we feel some affinity, becomes a process of deindividuation—that is, defining yourself as an individual whose identity reaches beyond family, community, and now history.

The process of deindividuation is fraught with many potential hazards and pitfalls. Persons who are deindividuated think for themselves. They make decisions based upon their particular needs and goals and *not* those of "the community" or "the people." As previously discussed, those persons who see little difference between their personal goals and black community goals are likely pathologically entangled in history and misplaced obligation. They see the process of becoming self-oriented as an abandonment of sorts, like leaving behind a soldier of the struggle and battle. But be absolutely certain of just who are your comrades-in-arms. This is a crucial step in the progression toward psychological freedom and in joining The Advancement. Are they advancers or delayers? Do they move forward or do they await deliverance? Enmeshed persons likely think their comrades-in-arms are both advancers *and* delayers. Wrong! Make no mistake about Pookie. His struggles are his own and of his own making.

Deindividuated persons become increasingly intolerant of Pookie's deleterious and self-defeating behavior. But many of us have become caught up in the romanticization of the relationship between advancers and delayers, likening the former to a vanguard of sorts. Whether called vanguard, shepherds, saviors, messiahs, the One, advancers, the talented tenth, the crème de la crème, or the chosen few, we have been charged with uplifting the people and leading the troops. But aren't troops supposed to be in a state of readiness? Aren't they trained to move forward and not simply wait to be carried?

I know my Pookie ain't worth the trouble. Just as you know your Pookies aren't worth it either. We know it in our hearts. They're unredeemable. Yet we still hold on 'cause he's our cousin, our brother, our nephew, our son. We hold on 'cause he's a black man. We remember when Pookie was young and had potential. Now he has young children spread over half the city. He's always

---

Scene: DAVISON FAMILY BARBECUE

Pookie: JD, let me borrow five dollars. I'll get it to you soon as I get back on my feet.

JD: Damn, Pookie! I can't even eat my ribs in peace without you beggin'. What you want, man?

Pookie: Five dollars. That's all. Just 'til I'm back on my feet.

JD (pausing to suck sauce off his fingers): Pookie, you been getting back on your feet for, let's see, twenty-five years! Boy, as far as I know you never was on your feet.

Pookie: Why you wanna front me off? No, I ain't all college educated and shit. I'm still out here struggling with my black people. No, I stayed home to help my people—black people—while you was at college getting too good for us. You best remember who you is!

JD (relenting to the struggling black people bullshit): Okay, Pookie. What you need five dollars for?

Pookie (pride and advantage regained): I need five dollars 'cause I'm a black man in America. You hear me? A black man!

---

wanting "a little somethin.'" It doesn't matter whether it's money, time, sex, or an audience. It has never been enough, and it will never be enough for Pookie to orchestrate his life beyond his own constrictions.

Fortunately, dumping Pookie is a relatively simple process:

DIRECTIONS (from a sitting position):
1. Firmly plant your feet.
2. Rise until you are standing fully erect.
3. Walk (briskly) out the nearest exit.

DIRECTIONS (from a standing position):
1. Walk (briskly) out the nearest exit.

DIRECTIONS (from a position of guilt, intimidation, shame, and obligation):
1. Firmly plant your feet.
2. Walk (briskly) out the nearest exit.

Many of us stay tied to Pookie as a result of habit. We let ourselves get used to his bullshit and that of a community intent on self-preservation. But black delayers such as Pookie forget that we are supposed to be in process. We are not static. We cannot maintain the same codependent and enmeshed relationship with them as they move backward. We're developing. We're in flux. We're moving forward. Pookie insists that we remember him despite his constrictive trap. The trap is of his own making. Apparently he likes it. Who am I to disturb his peace?

It is imperative that we dump Pookie. If not, his weight will surely drag us down. Not only will dumping him free us of the burden of carrying another, but it also challenges the very person who should bear the weight—Pookie.

Chapter 21

GIVE BACK TO THE BLACK COMMUNITY?

Gimme a Break!

The worst families are those in which the members never really speak their minds to one another; they maintain an atmosphere of unreality, and everyone always lives in an atmosphere of suppressed ill-feeling.
—WALTER BAGEHOT

Think of your forefathers! Think of your posterity!
—JOHN QUINCY ADAMS

Maybe it's me. Maybe I missed the day that all that outpouring of support from the black community happened. I could have been in the library on that day, studying so assiduously that I didn't hear the parade of support march by. I know when I'm trying to improve myself I can become a bit oblivious to things right outside my door or myself. Or perhaps I was at home, licking my wounds from the most recent run-in with the neighborhood street gang. I think someone must have neglected to tell them that we were in this together, and that they shouldn't try every single day to kick my ass for wanting more than a future of felony counts and early death. (To be fair, they did contribute to my fleetness of foot, and helped me learn to fight on days that I wasn't quite fleet enough.) Or perhaps I was at home trying to shake off the most recent assault to my psyche by the criminals, junkies, and hustlers of the neighborhood. They always seemed poised to derail the dreams of achieving children through the enticement of money, power, and rationalizations. Or perhaps I was sequestered in my own room, brain spinning wildly, trying to figure out why those few persons who could have been positive role models remained disgracefully mute while I and other children dealt with these neighborhood hazards every day. Who knows where I was, but it seems that I missed that day of black community support.

Maybe it's me, but I don't remember the community giving me any damned help from the beginning—at least not my immediate and present community. It seemed I was able to grow *despite* their "contributions." I believe that the community that is owed is not comprised of these charlatans, beggars, ne'er-do-wells, and users that we see on the streets every day. These delayers are not of any significance in the black struggle other than a place from which to launch. The community deserving of our attention is comprised of those persons who sacrificed for us. They came before us, and, given the constraints of their times, ran their lap in the race. That community—slaves, sharecroppers, Tuskegee Airmen, kitchen domestics, intellects, entrepreneurs, and other creative types—pushed the envelope. They are, in my opinion, deserving of the efforts of black advancers. That community deserves to be enlivened and honored through our efforts. These are the communities that deserve being given back to. And the giving back that needs to be done is simply continuing to strive and push the envelopes. I don't think our forebears would look kindly on efforts to enable black delayers who do little but sit on their asses waiting for deliverance. I know had I lived their lives and suffered their trials and indignities I would not countenance such brazen disregard. The present community is simply trying to count us among its resources—just another meal ticket or excuse not to try. Trying to race pimp us. Well, I won't be pimped. Sorry.

Really. Think about it. What did Willie the Wino, Jimmy the Junkie, or Hattie the Ho do for you other than provide a floor from which to measure your upward movement? What did they instill in you that launched you on your way other than provide examples of what not to emulate? I would think very little.

BLACK RAGS TO BLACK RICHES

I insist that there are two competing versions of the black community's contribution to the forward movement of advancers. Here's how the romanticized story goes: Darlene, a young black child, is brought up in a community considerably less affluent than middle class. She struggles with some school subjects, but her brightness shines through nonetheless. Darlene gets help from family, friends, and neighbors, because black Americans identify strongly with the idea that "it takes a community to raise a child." She applies herself, gets into college, graduates, and becomes very successful. Darlene returns to the community to help uplift her people and to show them the way. After all, Darlene is conscientious, and despite her newfound success, she remembers where she came from and how the black community bolstered and supported her.

Whether we're talking about *Roots*, *Uptown Saturday Night*, or a host of other entertainment vehicles, this notion of the returning, uplifting hero plagues black advancers. It plagues us because it is patently untrue for most of us. It is shameless romanticism, pure and simple. The notion is imaginary at best—but, more accurately, a fraud.

A more realistic and accurate depiction might go something like this: Darlene, a young black child, is brought up in a community considerably less affluent than middle class. (Here the stories diverge significantly and fatefully.) Darlene is bright, and if she is lucky perhaps one or two persons will recognize her potential and encourage her efforts. Darlene is often alone because she is perceived as weird since she chooses to study instead of partying, hanging out, and making overtures toward teenage pregnancy. Mostly, she is ridiculed for her disconnection from those sinking into a morass of their own design.

Darlene applies herself and learns to rely on her academic accomplishments for reinforcement. Despite a lack of support, she gets into college, graduates, and becomes very successful. Interestingly, when she returns to the community to visit, her few childhood supporters are the only ones who don't have their hands outstretched. It seems her accomplishments are their rewards, and they encourage her to continue as far as she can. However, all those attackers, detractors, and clowns from her childhood are lined up with their hands outstretched. Talking 'bout how she owes the community and should give back. The worst among them are actually waiting to be lifted up—almost bodily— out of their self-imposed pit.

Darlene reaches high levels in her career and her life because she is unencumbered by the weight of those waiting to be uplifted. For Darlene, lack of industry and preparation by black delayers fails to translate to a crisis of affiliation and philanthropy.

Historically, the treatment of black advancers has not been the supportive bed of roses romantically depicted. The discrepancy between romanticism and truth has had profound and reverberating effects upon the lives of black Americans. It serves to define the foundation for the increasing separation between black advancers and black delayers while offering explanation of the increasing intolerance and impatience of black advancers toward their supposedly downtrodden brethren. As well, it bodes a future where black delayers will, through continued sloth, poor motivation, and recalcitrance, bring about for themselves a new invisibility.[1]

For black advancers it is not self-hate or shame about who they are that drives a wedge between them and black delayers. To the contrary, these people have learned to love themselves *despite* the community's efforts to suggest they are wanting. Black advancers have instead embraced the boundlessness of their futures and rejected the lethargy and refuse of the community. They have become legitimized and, in essence, metamorphosed. They are new black females and new black males—unafraid to forge out on their own and be reckoned with. They are intolerant of limitations—whether from institutional sources or from the history and culture of the black community.

They are free!

Chapter 22

ABANDONING THE TRENCHES
Defeat and Misery in the 'Hood

All affectation is the vain and ridiculous attempt of poverty to appear rich.
—JOHANN KASPER LAVATER

Not in the clamor of the crowded street,
Not in the shouts and plaudits of the throng,
But in ourselves, are triumph and defeat.
—HENRY WADSWORTH LONGFELLOW

Once or twice a week after dinner my father would put his work boots on again and leave the house. He'd return after a few hours with the neatest things: an old but fixable (according to him) record player, a ten-year-old portable washing machine with two wheels missing, and countless lamps, televisions, and chairs. Metal objects and piles of magazines and newspapers made him most happy.

I believe my father had decided that he would be a father—that he would have a family and support it. In those days that meant he needed a hustle. Not in the nefarious sense of the word, but in its meaning of making money on the side through extra work. There was a time in black community life that a hustle was a good thing. People got some extra time at work, held a part-time job,

201

Scene. FORTY YEARS AGO. KITCHEN TABLE,
302 E. HAINES STREET

Little Jim: Where you going Daddy? Can I go?
Big Jim: No, you're still too young. I'm going junkin'.
Little Jim: When I be old 'nuf to go with you Daddy?
Big Jim (playfully): Let's see. How old are you now?
Little Jim: Ten.
Big Jim: Let me feel your muscle.
Little Jim (flexing his bicep): See!
Big Jim: Okay. After your next birthday.
Little Jim (bouncing joyfully): Mom, Daddy said I could start junkin' after my birthday.

delivered newspapers before going off to their regular jobs, went junkin', or did whatever legitimate thing they could do to support their families.

During those more innocent times, criminals in the 'hood were not quite as glamorized as they are today. Oh, we had criminals. The numbers runner and the dope man were present, but not prevalent. The persons who ran the local speakeasy were shady, but for the most part stayed in the shadows. Nefarious activities were done on the side, on the sly, and down low. But many of the men and women of my childhood worked—and worked hard. They were not afraid to work. They relished opportunities to "get ahead." In essence, they did whatever they needed to do to provide for their families. Lame excuses were for very, very weak persons. Respectability was king.

Responsibility for oneself seems the thing most lacking in the 'hood today. Excuses are rampant. Rationalizations are readily accepted. There's too much understanding and too much empathy. We tolerate way too much recounting of history—way too much. It seems few persons want to work hard, if at all. Everyone wants to be the man, but so few have passed adolescence. In fact, adolescence seems to be the benchmark that defines much of the 'hood. Kids run

Scene: TODAY. STREET CORNER,
RATIONALIZATION SESSION ABOUT TO BEGIN

Paul: I went over to that place like Pops told me, but they ain't paying nothin'.

Mom: What you mean they ain't payin' nothin'? Boy, them people got to be payin' somethin'. They ain't gonna have you workin' down there for nothin'.

Paul: Of course they payin' somethin'. It just ain't enough. Seven thirty-five an hour. I can't get ahead on that.

Mom (confused): How much you makin' now, Paul?

Paul: You gonna start that again, Mom?

Mom: I guess so, Paul.

Paul: I gotta make at least fifteen an hour to get what I need. I need a nice crib, a fly ride, and nice clothes. Plus, my cell phone bill is high.

our neighborhoods. Whether they are chronologically adolescent or mentally adolescent doesn't much matter: It is still the cult and character of the young that pervades our streets. It is the bravado of demanding respect on the streets or visiting violent retribution on those who dissed us that permeates the air we breathe. Hard hustle has supplanted hard work.

Many adult parents remain at home trying to retain a tenuous hold on their children. The streets beckon their kids and parents often feel ineffectual in fighting the power of today's watchwords:

"I gotta get mine."

"I gotta get paid."

"Jobs are for suckers."

"Anybody mess with mine gonna get smoked."

Such pronouncements must surely be frightening to any adult parent trying to rear children. Attempting to instill in one's children a work ethic and values beyond cash can be very difficult given the prevalent attitudes. Maybe you feel you are losing more battles as your child comes home later and later. Or your daughter brings her newborn baby home for you to provide primary care. These standards of the adolescent culture cannot be tolerated long without destroying the fabric of our families and communities. I fear it may be too late to reverse the tide. So get out of the way of oncoming waves. Move yourself and your family *out the 'hood*.

They are your children and grandchildren. I would not let allegiance to a false sense of family, community, or blackness deter me from taking care of my children. Do not surrender them and yourself to the streets. Take charge. Take control. Empower yourself.

Chapter 23

SNAKEBITE
Surviving the Venom

The happiness of others is never bearable for very long.
—Françoise Sagan

Misery not only loves company, it insists on it.
—Old Folk Saying

So you've decided to take the leap toward psychological freedom. Guess what? Your leap will not be appreciated by everyone. It's a fact. Some people will show interest but remain standoffish, not knowing how to deal with the changes in you. Others will be foreboding, expecting some unknown evil as you pursue an unshepherded life. Still others will react with anger and venom. What is likely angering them are envy and frustration related to their own lack of fortitude in moving toward psychological freedom. How dare you move on and advance without them? How dare you consider a future defined by you and you alone? Your critics are snakes—venomous and bewitching. They are miserable that you are increasingly resistant to their poison and growing away from them. Miserable! You feel me? They are miserable that you are blossoming. And, not unlike an emotionally abusive partner, they are afraid that you will leave. If you really think about it, they've always been miserable, restrictive of themselves and others. They are miserable—and you know what they say about misery.

Scene: THREE FRIENDS AT REE-REE'S BEAUTY SHOP

Brenda: Tamika, I know Tasha's lying, but she said you said you was too busy to hang out Friday night. Tell me her ass is lying.

Tamika: I told y'all before. I got a class Saturday morning. I got to hit the books. Plus, y'all hang out too damn late anyway.

Tasha: Told ya!

Brenda: Oh, we was good 'nuf fo' your ass before you started going up to that college and getting all saddity.

Tamika: I'm not being saddity. I'm just taking a class. I'm trying to do something for me and my son.

Brenda: So what you tryin' to say? We all got some damn sons! I know you ain't tryin' to say I don't do nothing for Little Man-Man. Oh, hell no! I know you ain't trying to say that!

Tamika: Look. School's over next month. After that, I can hang with y'all all night if you want.

Brenda: Naw. I ain't hardly tryin' to hear that. Friday night is tomorrow. Not next month. And not after school's over. You our homegirl or not?

Tamika: Yeah, we're homegirls. But, we ain't been out for almost six months, anyway. How come it can't wait 'til school's done?

Brenda: Look, you got to decide. Your homegirls or some lame-ass college people. Keep it real. You know what I'm saying?

(Brenda turns to Tasha for a high-five.)

Actually, it's pretty ironic that personal growth in black communities is sometimes treated with disdain. After all, other black persons should be happy for you, happy for all of us. They are supposed to be our brothers and sisters. Right? Part of our black family at large. Right? Where's the love? Aren't family members supposed to be happy for other family members as they improve? Or am I just missing the point?

One of the well-accepted themes of dysfunctional families is related to the maintenance of unhealthy relationships. Generally, as individual family members become less enmeshed and more healthy psychologically, other members deteriorate and demonstrate increasingly destructive and negative behaviors. While dysfunctional, these behaviors are in the service of maintaining familiar patterns of interaction and pulling the improving family member back into the web. Like crabs in a basket, they pull back any of their kind who try to escape.

One of my private practice clients once remarked how shocked and then angry she had become when her "friends and family" showed their lack of appreciation for the change she had made in her life:

> Dr. Davison, they showed their ass. I spent years of my time and thousands of dollars with my friends. Some of these people I've known since we were kids. But the moment I decided to do something for me, they got really funky. Told me I was being Miss Anne. That I had forgot I was black. They even had the nerve to threaten me, saying that if I couldn't keep it real, then I couldn't hang with them anymore. To go be with my white friends. But do you know what I said to them Dr. Davison? Do you? I told them I hadn't forgotten I was black, but they had sure forgotten I was human.

Rekindling the light of our humanity after nearly four hundred years of extinguished essence and darkened visions will take work. But it is crucial and sacred work—for ourselves, for our kids, for our forebears, for the world. We are more than black men and black women. We have souls and psyches and personal dynamics. We possess egos and selves and lives. And, as a result of these attributes, *we differ from one another*. No longer should *black* define and shape you. *You* should shape you.

During my own journey toward psychological freedom, I often relished being seen as different. It usually meant I was on the right track and had moved beyond the boundaries and influence of the black border patrol. This was important to me because of all the misery I saw around me. Had I succumbed to the venom of the snakes, I too would now be invested in the subjugation of black men and women. I too could be a member of the black border patrol.

You must inoculate yourself against the scourge of black unanimity. It is

> Scene: MONTHLY MEETING OF THE
> BLACK BORDER PATROL
>
> Chairperson: I'd like to call this meeting of the BBP to order. Any new business?
> Field Agent: Yes, Chairperson. I'd like to report that I saw Toni Robertson at Big Slim's Record Shoppe. You know we've been surveilling her ever since that Barbra Streisand incident. Yesterday I witnessed her purchasing tickets for *La Boheme*.
> (Gasps heard around the room.)
> Chairperson: You mean . . . ?!
> Field Agent: Yes. I'm afraid so. She's going to see an opera.
> (Woman near back of room rises, then faints over her neighbors.)
> Chairperson (heatedly): Someone's gotta talk to the sister, and tell her to keep it real before it's too late! My Lord! Any other business?
> Sister Keisha: Yes, Chairperson. The CRAP (Committee for the Retention of African American Pride) has selected a new motto that we unanimously feel reflects our mission. It is, "Why should you be happy?"
> Chairman: Very good, Sister Keisha! Very good indeed.

evil magic that causes one to suggest that dissent from popular but antiquated beliefs is traitorous. The inoculation begins by knowing and understanding the snakes that desire to bite you. You know them already. Sometimes they parade around in dashikis and Kente cloth—stuck in a time warp (and poorly dressed). Sometimes they just sit around thinking they know what's good for you, for them, for everybody. They never stray too far from the community unless in the service of finding new victims. They think themselves somehow better, nobler, and more relevant than the rest of us. They overestimate the white man's evil while underestimating the resolve of black men and women.

Avoid the snakes who would bite you, infect you, and drag you backward. Give them less importance and influence in your life. After all, you're grown. Do you really need their conditional support, their guilt, their shame? Remember where you are going. If your friends and family can't stand beside you and support your dreams, then dump them. Don't get distracted by their purportedly nobler causes. Your battles are yours.

Mercifully, you don't have to do any of this alone. One of our black community fables is that of the black individual forging out alone without support or role models. Support is all around you. No, you won't find it at Ree-Ree's Beauty Shop or at Big Poppa's Biscuits and Bar-B-Que. It's on buses bound for college campuses. It's in libraries, in museums, on talk radio shows, and in bookstores. It's in monthly book clubs, at PTA meetings, at Girl Scout and Boy Scout gatherings, and in GED classes. Supportive persons are much more plentiful than you think. Step out and away from the snakes. Seek safer and more solid ground. Find smarter and more motivated persons. Cherish those black advancers who cross your path. They're not Uncle Toms—they're beacons on your journey toward psychological freedom.

Anger and venom are to be expected as you separate from traditional black community standards and edicts. Strategies for guarding yourself against attacks to your character, motivations, and intentions will be indispensable. Be sure to establish supportive affiliations toward self-esteem enhancement and emotional protection. Make no mistake about it. You are entering a war, a pitched battle between black advancers and black delayers as they seek to define the direction of black America. The prize is your soul and your future. Toward which perspective will you align?

Chapter 24

Deal with yourself as an individual worthy of respect and make everyone else deal with you the same way.
—Nikki Giovanni

Why not go out on a limb? Isn't that where the fruit is?
—Frank Scully

For black individuals who have chosen to live nonsanctioned lives, identity concerns are a recurring quagmire. Such persons, due to their rejection of the limited range of careers and lifestyles, have rarely been supported by black communities. More rarely, because of their damnable blackness and audacity, have such persons been accepted by white communities. This sense of feeling between two worlds causes a feeling of marginality—fitting in neither place—that often exists for black advancers.

Traditionally, black advancers (e.g., scholars, artists, inventors) had to live their lives marginalized. White folks were unaccepting and suppressive of their efforts, while black folks were puzzled, but also unaccepting. Lack of acceptance defined the margin, and these advancers often had to learn to provide their own reinforcement for their efforts. Encouraging smiles and pats on the back were not forthcoming. There was little—and sometimes no—support

Scene: TWO FRIENDS BUMPING INTO EACH OTHER
ON THE STREET

Bill: Hey man. My woman says she saw you couple days ago over to the Y. Carrying some kind of tanks or something. You got a new job? They hiring?

Thomas (cautiously): No. I'm just finishing up a class.

Bill: Oh yeah? In what?

Thomas: Scuba.

Bill: Scuba?! You mean like bloop . . . bloop . . . bloop? Underwater scuba?

Thomas (impatiently): Yeah, Bill. That's where most scuba takes place. Underwater.

Bill (smirking): Man, you crazy! Scuba diving? What you doing that for? Brother, black folks don't be doing no scuba diving. For what? I'd pay good money to see your black ass down there, looking like some chocolate Jack Kudo. Probably scaring the hell out the fish 'cause I *know* they ain't never seen no black scuba diver.

Thomas: It's Jacques Cousteau.

Bill: Whatever. That ain't the point. Scuba?! That's white people's shit.

Thomas: Whatever, man. I got to get gone.

Bill: Hell, man. If you gonna be doing that scuba anyway, maybe we could turn a profit or something. I'm gonna give that some thought. Meantime, next time you down there could you get me some catfish or some shrimp? I loves me some fried catfish and shrimp!

(Thomas, exasperated, remains silent. Bill walks away in roaring laughter.)

coming from their families and friends. Sometimes their efforts were met only with derision. Too often, for their toil, they died in anonymity.

Now, black advancers enjoy a wholly different venue for their achievements. Slowly, the margin has changed. Wherever you go, and whatever you do, you will find other black persons already there or on the road with you. Rarely are there any more black firsts. As an advancer, you will not be entering areas unchartered and untraveled, just areas largely unendorsed and unaccepted by black popular perspective. This concept of marginality is not a phenomenon to be trivialized. The importance of its meaning for black advancers cannot be overstated. More than a few advancers have been defeated by the specter of marginality. Weakness and a susceptibility of their egos to black unanimity of thought was a death knell to scores of black advancers. Not fitting in somewhere—anywhere—was the downfall of many persons who set off to new horizons. The death of marginality marked an important juncture for black Americans. It signaled acceptance by persons on all sides of the racial divide. Skills and character—not race—have become primary and paramount in human exchange. Being as you desire, thinking as you desire, and behaving as you desire are indicators of increasing psychological freedom.

We black advancers are no longer our companies' only—at one time castigated as "token"—black scientists or black architects. We are often our companies' best scientists or best architects, qualified not by race or ethnicity but by our acquired skills and our mastery over institutionalized challenges that make us stars. This is an amazing and momentous achievement for black Americans. It speaks to Dr. King's invoking of "content of our character." Let's not move backward while maintaining an erroneous assumption of racial identity and heritage. That's dead—and with it, marginality.

Because . . .

A. Philip Randolph organized the first march on Washington.
Ralph J. Bunche won a Nobel Peace Prize.
James Meredith matriculated at Ole Miss.
David Walker wrote an *Appeal*.
Adam Clayton Powell was outspoken.

Mary McCleod Bethune advised a president.

Shirley Chisholm sought the presidency.

In 1877 Henry Flipper mastered the Point.

Sixty-four years and four enemy aircraft later, Dorrie Miller still had to return to the mess hall.

Charles Lenox Redmond and Frederick Douglass were able to disagree.

Hiram Rhodes Revels served in Congress.

Blanche K. Bruce wasn't far behind Hiram.

W. E. B. Du Bois looked forward.

Booker T. Washington stood up.

Thurgood Marshall knew the law.

Paul Robeson also had a law degree.

York, unafraid of the wilderness, traveled with Lewis and Clark.

Matthew Henson was unafraid of the cold.

Jean Baptiste Point du Sable had an outpost—Chicago.

The *Chicago Defender* was so much more than a rag.

Nat Love (Deadwood Dick) was a cowboy extraordinaire.

Crispus Attucks refused to back down.

Paul Cuffee helped free blacks return to Africa.

William Sill conducted in Philadelphia.

Germantown, Pennsylvania, has much more than a few cobblestones to be proud of.

Angela Davis was first a graduate student.

Benjamin Banneker wrote a scientific book.

Thomas Jennings received a patent.

Elijah McCoy was the Real McCoy.

George Washington Carver was a scientist.

Bessie Coleman had wings.

The Tuskegee Airmen flew like eagles.

Col. Guion Bluford, Dr. Mae C. Jemison, and Dr. Ronald McNair learned to soar.

Marian Anderson sang so beautifully.

Chapter 25

OF SOFT PRETZELS, CHERRY WATER ICE, AND HOAGIES

Courage is not simply *one* of the virtues but the form of every virtue at the testing point.
—CYRIL CONNOLLY

The time is always right to do what is right.
—MARTIN LUTHER KING JR.

Dear William,

Ever since your recent flap with the delayers, I have felt terrible for not being there for you during their ranting. I know facing such crab beds can be daunting, particularly when people vehemently attack you for what they see in their mirrors but are too afraid to address. Although I was indisposed at the time of your difficulties, addressing delayers of my own, there is really little excuse. Too many of we advancers fail to stand strong with our brethren against the onslaught of fear. For my absence during your trials I would like to formally apologize. Upon reflection I discovered several compelling reasons why I, more than most persons, should have had your back covered.

First and foremost are our common roots. You are probably not aware of it, but we're damned near homeboys. You and I are from the same city and went to the same schools. We both attended Central and Temple (Go Lancers! Go Owls!). I think we even share Germantown in common, although you walked its streets and alleys some years before I did. Man, with this much connection, we should have been talking a long time ago. Maybe you should have called, William. Us Philadelphia boys, we gotta stick together. One of the redeeming values of being native sons of such a unique metropolis is access to a rather extensive range of homies. The next time these delayers come trying to sell wolf tickets, we'll cash them together. Let 'em come with it! Next time, we'll be waitin' on 'em—them and their weak-assed arguments. But I digress. Back to coverage of your back.

The second reason I should have been there for you is related to family. My mother, who is considered by many to be the pope of Germantown (I know. I saw the white smoke myself!), claims she knew your people. But who really knows? I question her memory as she also claims to have known Chubby Checker's mom, kibitzed with Tammi Terrell, and watched little Teddy Pendergast grow up. Man, a lot of good singing talent came out of that section of the city. Can you sing, William? How much stoop time did you put in?

The third reason I should have been there for you is that I am a psychologist. I think this helps me understand why delayers go crazy when asked to look in the mirror. They have deluded themselves into the belief that the system is doing little for them. They feel entitled and somehow justified in their inertia and motivational laze. And now many advancers—in their opinion, true "haters of the game"—are telling them to get themselves together. How dare we advancers ask them to now show a speck of the fortitude displayed by their enslaved or sharecropping or beaten-down or uneducated and unopportuned forebears?

I don't know if it was the same during your era, but on the streets of my Germantown, having heart was considered one of the more important attributes among the fellas. Hearing someone say, "The boy don't got no heart" or "He's a punk to his heart" would be a death knell for the homie in question. No respect from the fellas. No play from the girls. No action of any kind. A fight would break out pretty quickly when those words were spoken to your face.

I think that is much of the problem today. Delayers don't got no heart, and people like you and me—we're calling them out. No wonder they want to fight. But William, I'm down with you. If they want to go, then let's go. My motivation for challenging black delayers is not for my own purposes, but to recognize and honor the efforts of those black Americans who went before us. How dare delayers sit back when our forebears stood firm in the face of unspeakable crimes against humanity and endured indignities atop indignities? We owe them advancement. We owe them this fight.

My father and his father had heart. In fact, the overwhelming majority of adults I grew up around had heart. Not a lot of opportunities were there for them, but they made the best they could with what they had. As you and I did also. I hear a lot of complaining these days, but I witness very little heart.

What presents as most unnerving for me are accusations of being a sellout or an Uncle Tom or hating myself. These delayers are so very wrong. Their sense of entitlement blinds them to one of the basic facts of life: that is, no one owes you anything except yourself. Our fathers and mothers knew that. You and I and many of our peers learned that. Why don't these people know that too? Or are they simply trying to get over? Sometimes, William, I find myself filling with indifference to their plight. How 'bout you?

For your information, things in Germantown have changed a lot, and in some ways things have stayed the same. You can still get a very good cheesesteak or hoagie just about anywhere in the area. Except Fat's on Germantown Avenue closed down. When I heard this fact I was, as I'm sure you are now, crushed. I cannot, for the life of me, remember that black lady's name who worked there, but she could fix an Italian hoagie that would make you hurt yourself. Even the Italian homies from South Philly would have appreciated her unequaled culinary skills. In fact, I think I once saw some Italian guys cruising the Avenue in search of Fat's.

Remember the 23 running up and down the tracks and cobblestones of Germantown Avenue? SEPTA changed it to a regular bus instead of a trolley so they wouldn't get so tangled up. If you will recall, people parking their cars too close to the tracks or the simple mechanical breakdown of just one trolley would bring the Avenue to a standstill for miles. You know, it's almost a shame there are buses now. I kinda liked it when eight or nine trolleys got stuck behind one that couldn't move forward. Then suddenly they'd become untangled and start rolling toward their waiting patrons. But with shift change fast approaching, the trolleys would fly past each transit stop as if people hadn't been waiting for forty-five or fifty minutes. It always made me smile to hear the old ladies cussin'.

Do you remember that one dude who walked around Germantown drunk all the time? I think they called him Music. He died. I was also told that the Haines Street and Dogtown gangs still exist, but who knows for sure? My source was an old Hype I encountered while waiting on the 23. And that one family that thought they ran Germantown is still around. But no honor remains, man; only drug dealers and drug users.

Do you remember?

When I die
bury me deep;
deep in the heart
of old Haines Street.

I remember when that used to be cool. Adolescent male posturing I guess is what the educators and psychologists would call it now.

Vernon Park's still there. Although the last time I walked through the junkies had taken over. Man, my mother used to tell me stories about summer evenings when she and her girlfriend would push their baby strollers through that park. Not no more, bro. Not no more.

Well, William, I must close for now. Delayers await! I hope this correspondence finds you and your family in good health and spirits. Take care of yourself and those you love. Remember homie, next time without a doubt I got your back.

Be cool.

JD

Chapter 26

THE OTHER SIDE OF THE MOUNTAIN
Black Identity beyond The Struggle

The highest goal of mankind is the liberty of the individual.
—ERNEST RENAN

While there is a place for racial identities in a world shaped by racism . . . if
we are to move beyond racism, we shall have, in the end, to move beyond current racial identities.
—ANTHONY APPIAH

One of the most engaging dilemmas of a long, arduous struggle *is knowing and appreciating when the end is upon you.* Most black persons of my generation are very familiar with the idea of "keep on keeping on." Its suggestion of perseverance and fortitude were good for soul and mind. We struggled and fought through a horrendous history, a history unique in its brutality and powerful in its enduring aftereffects. The phenomenon of always struggling, always climbing, and always moving forward is as much a part of our history as the plantations from which our journeys were launched. Struggles and obstacles have been so much a part of our history that many persons feel incapable of disengaging from their past and moving toward their futures.

I remember my own struggles through school. Studying, planning, preparing for challenges. Like any war or struggle, attrition is wearying, for

Scene: THE EVENING OF NATHAN JR.'S
COLLEGE GRADUATION

Big Momma: You been blessed, Nathan. You got to go to college, and now you're graduated and about to start out your life. My little Boo's a man today! What you planning to do first?

Kellie (Nathan's sister, interrupting sarcastically): Your little Boo should be using his education to help some of these folks 'round here, instead of trippin'.

Nathan: Shut up, Kellie!

Big Momma: What's she talking 'bout Nathan?

Nathan: Big Momma, I don't mean no disrespect, but these people don't need my education or my energy. What they need is motivation, and they need to get off their butts. Putting my time and energy into that hole is a waste. Ask Malcolm X and Dr. King.

Big Momma: A waste?! Boy if I knew you'd be talking like this when you got grown . . . Lord, Jesus! Boy, ain't nothing wasteful helping someone who ain't got much as you. I raised you to have good sense. And now you done gone got a good education, but you ain't showing no good sense. Boy, you could help a whole lotta folks who don't got what you got. And I don't want to never hear you talkin' poorly 'bout Reverend King again!

Nathan: But, Big Momma, the reason they don't have what I

both the attacker and the attacked. But when it's done, it's done. And guess what folks? We're done! We've reached the mountaintop! And beyond! Our new challenges are many, but personal. The hills and mounds we now face are ours individually. There no longer exist mountains that we're all climbing together. We've already reached the summits, and the view is an expanse of small hills and mounds to be faced by black persons as individuals.

have is they don't want to work for what I have. Them people up at that college didn't just *give* me a degree. I earned it, Big Momma! I worked and studied every single day 'til I got it. Weekdays, weekends, every day! Let them get off their butts and work too. Just like I did.

Big Momma: Nathan Jr., I can't believe you talking like that. There's a lot of folks out there who ain't been blessed like you. Black folks always needing smart people like you to help out.

Nathan: Big Momma, there's plenty of other smart people who probably would be more than happy to help out. That's just not for me. I'm going for mine.

Kellie: Tell Big Momma what you're going to do. Fool! Tell her!

Nathan: Big Momma, I signed up for a year for a ranch job in Montana to decide what it is I want to do.

Big Momma: Montana?!

Kellie: That's right, Big Momma. Montana. Where the deer and the antelope play. Boy, what exactly is your problem? I told y'all years ago something was wrong with Nathan, but I just got smacked. The boy's got issues. Look, fool! Your place is here with us and our neighbors and our friends. Not in Montana chasing buffalo or whatever. You really need to keep it real, Nathan!

Nathan: No! My place is where I feel I need to be. Doing what I need to do for me. That's keeping it real!!

Our first mountain was conquered in 1863, the year of our emancipation. It was scaled for physical freedom, release from the shackles and chains of enslavement. Our second mountain was conquered one hundred years later, in 1965, the year of the Voting Rights Act. It was scaled for political freedom, release from the indignities and inequalities of second-class citizenry.[1]

The scaling of our third mountain—psychological freedom—in my opinion, was marked by the Clarence Thomas confirmation hearings. Not only was a divergence of black thought (conservatism) given forum and voice, but on an international stage two black persons were presented as intelligent, but unsupportive of each other and at odds.[2]

Folks, there are no more mountains! We must now learn to walk toward the fertile fields and glens our forebears envisioned for us. Inclusion and dispersion throughout the American fabric is our destiny—in factories, courthouses, pig farms, legislatures, and boardrooms—everywhere.

YOU BEYOND BLACK

Who are you? What makes you tick? How do you know you are you? Many persons define themselves by the things they do: "I'm an architect, a teacher, a police detective. I like to dance. I love camping. Foreign films are my passion." When you are asked who you are, does race, like an unconscious reflex, automatically come to mind? Do you say or begin with "I'm a black man" or "I'm a black woman"? And if you do, what else are you? Can black individuals only define themselves primarily by their racial and historical heritage? My point is this: Do not restrict your sense of self to *black* because you're feeling angry, entitled, or recalcitrant in reaction to historical oppression. Worse, do not remain embroiled—stuck—in a never-ending war for racial parity in deference to those black persons too dysfunctional to move forward. Do not permit history to define, determine, and limit you as an individual.

I move forward because my forebears could not. I soar because my forebears could not. I encourage my beautiful children to explore nonblack worlds because my forebears could not do so for their beautiful children. We are their legacy and this is our duty. The visions set for us by our forebears who *could not do* should not be darkened by black delayers who *will not do*. America's historical treatment of its black citizens should embolden us toward individual progress rather than ensnare us in angry and entitled group dysfunction.

ENCOURAGING BLACK IDENTITY
BEYOND THE STRUGGLE

Sometimes it's scary letting our children go where few of us have gone. But if my children are to advance, then I must become comfortable with the unknown. Our forebears did. You tell me what's more unknown and scary than nocturnal and beleaguered escape through swamps and forests toward freedom—hounds at their heels, lynch rope and shackles at the ready, death in the air? And because of what my forebears did, I am who I am, and I do what I do.

No longer can we live our *individual* lives chained to the history of black Americans as a group. Have you had ideas, thoughts, or desires that you squashed simply because they seemed at odds with what a *brother* or *sister* would do? Have you considered downhill skiing, scuba diving, or mountain trekking, but dismissed it in favor of "staying black"? Have you contemplated a cooking class or a relationship with a nonblack person, but deferred in the name of racial homogeneity? Have you thought about simply stopping along the roadside to smell the flowers or sitting idly in a park watching squirrels and pigeons, but opted to "keep it real"? The limiting box that has defined black America has been under constant pressure and change. We've been slaves, sharecroppers, porters, nannies, housekeepers, and pickaninnies. We've been separatists, integrationists, pacifists, militants, and pan-Africanists. We've been niggers, coloreds, Negroes, Afro-Americans, brothers and sisters, blacks, and African Americans. Are we ready now to just be our individual selves?

How does one come to know oneself without the struggle? Having finally arrived at the other side of the mountain, how do we allow ourselves variability and range beyond *black*? The answer is that we must now turn away from our leaders and toward ourselves. We must develop who we are beyond the struggle. Our great grandparents sharecropped and only whispered of equal playing fields. Our grandparents were part of a generation that endured and became victims of police dogs, water hoses, and intimidation. Our parents came north as part of the Great Migration and settled in urban settings. We have benefited from all their efforts. Now it is upon us to take the next courageous step forward. We *must* take that step forward. That step, I believe, is living the lives that our forebears worked so hard for us to have—that is, to be treated as normal persons with normal goals and without the denotations and connotations of racial disharmony. You feeling me? From their group, from our group, and from ourselves individually, we must insist on recognition of our idiosyncratic personhoods. That our lives are our own! They don't belong to others—black, white, otherwise—bent on forwarding their particular racial agenda. Our lives belong to us. We must blossom despite all their racial designs to keep us closed and entrenched in the struggle.

Many of us are already living those lives—purchasing homes outside the 'hood, educating our children without Eurocentricity or Afrocentricity, and maintaining high-quality friendships beyond race. More important, we develop ourselves—growing, feeling, thinking, acting, and loving without racial qualification and without censure.

We must move *beyond* race. Our *black identity* is a by-product of slavery and racism—an affectation, assumed rather than natural. Ideally, there should exist no such thing as black identity. It is part of our oppression, a notion propagated by those motivated to provide anchor to a people set adrift by slavery. I contend that that same anchor now ties us down, retarding our free movement. Freedom—that same goal that bound us together for the majority of our time in the United States—now threatens to split us forever apart. And that's a good thing! The schism that has always existed between black advancers and black delayers has become increasingly evident. Recognition and highlighting of that split will likely be painful, but any psychological growth is associated with painful release of that which is familiar. As a group, we've attained physical and political freedom: now on to psychological freedom and mental health outside the group.

The racial struggle, for many of us, is over. Our struggles are now centered around schools for our children, career opportunities, and development of self. Racial struggles are increasingly becoming secondary or tertiary concerns in our everyday discourse. Are *you* ready? Are *they* ready? Am *I* ready to just be me?

Chapter 27
EMBRACING THE NEW YOU

It takes a deep commitment to change and an even deeper commitment to grow.
—RALPH ELLISON

Growth itself contains the germ of happiness.
—PEARL BUCK

WARNING! WARNING! YOU HAVE JUST ENTERED A FREEDOM ZONE!

Nurturance and development of yourself beyond race represents the final objective for the descendants of African black slaves. It's the closing measure of our long journey to freedom, the conclusion of the struggle for black Americans. This final step also embodies the legacy of millions of souls reduced to huddled and dying black cargo in the holds of slave ships. Our ascension is their restoration. By embracing self beyond race, we need no longer *think* in black, *behave* in black, and *exist* in black. We need only be our individual selves, potent and absolute.

Together, we black Americans have gone through many racial passages. We have been slaves, sharecroppers, credits to our race, ingratiating sheep, militant lions, strugglers, and survivors. Now it's time to be much more. It's time for us to transcend the limitations and connotations of race. It's time for us—as individuals—to regain, in full, our humanity.

We must, with all deliberateness, close this monstrous history of racial limitation. We are *individuals.* That history of being defined and limited first by our oppressors, then by our community, and finally by ourselves is done. Nurturance of our individualities beyond race constitutes the long-awaited cessation of oppression for black persons. The realization of psychological freedom also heralds the ascension of new black persons over those hobbled and trapped by race.

BECOMING NEW

In order to move beyond the traps and limitations of race, you must first become new. You must learn to foster, accept, and embrace a new you. But how does a person become new? How do you transform yourself from a life marked by black conscription to an individual life totally of your own? How do you assert yourself as an unaligned and free person, no longer one group's stereotype and another's role model? And, given the social and personal prices to be paid, do you dare try to become new?

Hazards to Newness

The psychological barriers against becoming new extend far beyond our present lives and into the souls and essences of our forebears. America's history of racial oppression, community, and cultural traditions that aggrandize *black* identity, the overinclusiveness of the black family at large, keeping it real, enmeshment, and codependency all affect how many of us have remained unchanged in a world constantly in flux. Drenched and soaked in time, in pain, and in anguish, these psychological barriers await us as we pursue our ultimate and final freedom.

Fortunately, becoming new is not group activity. It is idiosyncratic. New-ness is a process specific to us as individuals. We need not wait for the entirety of black America to ready itself for the transformation. The misperception that our black family at large must rise up together compromises efforts toward newness. This final step of freedom, we black Americans take alone and indi-vidually, together only in spirit. For each individual the process will be dif-ferent. But before we discuss the *how* of becoming new, we must first address the *why* and its importance.

Our Finest Effort

Slavery and its long-term effects on society have put upon black individuals a racial imperative—an obligation to realize our fullest individual potential. To those black persons (e.g., slaves and sharecroppers) whose lives and dreams were crushed under the weight of racial limitation, we owe passage in this sailing toward psychological freedom. We must, in spirit, remove the master's heel from their necks and help them rise up. Bottom line: realization of our fullest economic, social, and psychological potential is what we owe ourselves and what we owe our forebears. This marks our racial imperative. And nothing—not another group's opinions, other black Americans (i.e., delayers), or even ourselves—should slow this movement. Too many lives have been spent and too many sacrifices have been made to get us to this point in history. Our imperative is simply too important to address in a cavalier and outdated fashion. That is the *why* of the matter.

However, let's be sure to recognize the full sweep of racial limitation. The crushing of lives, dreams, and spirits has come not only from outside the black community; it has come, as well, from inside its confines. Unquestioned obe-dience and allegiance to our parents, our community, Big Momma, the good reverend, ad infinitum are traditions steeped in the constrictions of the past. These traditions have served to squelch a sense of industry and social compe-tence among us as children. Lest we suffered whippings, we learned to mind elders who were ill equipped or disinclined to expand our minds and outlooks. An important part of becoming new includes reparenting ourselves away from the vestiges of slavery and toward the initiative, autonomy, and self-reliance needed today.

The mission each of us undertakes toward newness is momentous for ourselves but critical in validation of our forebears' efforts. In the traditions of Sojourner Truth and Frederick Douglass we carry these spiritual brothers and sisters forward with us. Learning to dump our present-day losers will also ease our burden. Actually, we should feel almost obligated to dump them. Ridding ourselves of their weight in order to complete the journey for ourselves and for our forebears is warranted—historically and psychologically.

Seeking to advance ourselves by nurturing and developing self beyond race is not forgetting of our spiritual brothers and sisters—at least not the ones who have chosen to move forward. Similarly, there is no forsaking of black heritage. To the contrary, it is advancement—undeterred and unremitting—that defines and characterizes the heritage of black Americans. However, heritage itself is passive, something to be reflected upon from an historical perspective. Although informative, the recounting of heritage is nonetheless a passive chore. One need do little more than recount heritage and teach it to the next generation.

Legacy, on the other hand, is active. It is history and future combined. Legacy is a pursuit and a continuance of a theme. For black advancers, this theme has always been and continues to be marked by freedom and potential pursued. Black heritage, while important, eventually becomes as stale as any other recounting of events and people. How many times, for example, must I hear Martin Luther King Jr.'s "I Have a Dream" speech? It is unquestionably an important part of our heritage, but nearly half a century has passed since it was delivered. Of course the speech has historical significance. But what have black people done since? That's the question of legacy. Legacy is dynamic and fresh—evolving constantly and setting the stage for those who follow. In many ways legacy is unknown and thereby unfettered. This is what we must transform our efforts toward: legacy over heritage, advancer over delayer.

Moreover, given the abundance of opportunities available to black persons in the United States today, it is criminal to rise only to complain or beg for help. Truly, it is sacrilege to the memories of those who came before us. They have earned and deserve our finest efforts. Now, given the *why*, let's become new.

Becoming new requires an awakening of sorts—a shift in *consciousness*—a transformation. Facing oneself, facing the world, empowerment, fearlessness, and orientation—backward or forward—all together constitute a *new consciousness*. It is this new consciousness that delivers us beyond race.

FACING ONESELF

Glad to Meet *You*

How do you welcome your new self? How do you say hello, maybe for the very first time, to *you*? The thought is probably a bit scary. You have, after all, come to be very comfortable with how you've been. You're familiar to you, even if you're not happy with you. You know you, just like you know that raggedy shirt you should have tossed out years ago or that old boyfriend or girlfriend you kept around way too long. People and things become comfortable for us because they're familiar. We're going to change all that. So let's begin the process of becoming new by getting a bit uncomfortable. That is truly how change happens: through feelings of discomfort or disequilibrium. It won't hurt—much.

Taking Inventory

Reflecting on your strengths and your weaknesses is a very important step toward becoming new. What are the things you do well and with little effort, and what are the things you struggle with? How can you turn your weaknesses into strengths? Next, look at who or what is helping you and who or what is getting in your way. Don't hesitate to list them all. And don't act like you can't complete this particular act of becoming new. If you are having trouble distinguishing the people and things that are good for you from those that are not, then perhaps denial should be listed first on your inventory. Be as brutally honest with yourself as possible. It will take some time and effort to clear yourself of the personal and societal distractions that estrange you from your true self.

Mirror, Mirror, on the Wall

Find a quiet space in your home where you will be left undisturbed. Tell your family or roommates to leave you alone for a while. That space might be a bedroom, a bathroom, or even a closet—anyplace that you will be by yourself, undisturbed. Look at yourself in a mirror. Really, *really* look at yourself. It might seem silly at first, but trust me. Soon enough it will have a telling effect. Think about what it is you want in life. Do you have it now? If not, are you even moving toward what you want in life? Will you ever move toward it? What or who gets in your way? Don't be afraid to look in the mirror and ask yourself hard questions. Don't shy away from your own image. People who are content with their lives and following the correct roads for themselves have little trouble maintaining eye contact with themselves.

During your alone time, learn to feel yourself. Close your eyes and feel your heart beating. Feel the blood coursing through your body. Listen to your breathing. Measure its rhythm. Let your neck, then your shoulders, then your arms relax. Feel the tension leave your hands. As your breathing slows, continue your relaxation process by concentrating on your legs. Let your thighs, then your lower legs, then your ankles relax. Feel your feet relaxing and the tension leaving your toes. Being in touch with the physical as well as the mental aspects of yourself will move you toward increased consciousness and the knowledge of who you are, which is the basis for becoming new.

It is this concept of self-knowledge that is so very often underdeveloped and unexpressed in our psyches. As slaves we were stripped of our humanity and individuality. In reaction to this era and other dehumanizing periods, we sought respect *as a race*. We highlighted positive aspects of ourselves *as a people*, while largely neglecting ourselves *as individuals*. Instead of expanding knowledge of our individual selves, knowledge of black history and The Struggle became our focus. This was important during those dehumanizing times. However, today's rehashing of our history and struggle can become atrophic, if not boring. Moreover, for the impotent, such rehashing fails to enact anything other than anger. Although knowledge of our history and The Struggle honors the past, it is knowledge of our individual selves that is the basis of The Advancement and becoming new.

Facing oneself can be an extremely difficult but rewarding task. When facing others, we simply don our black faces—our masks—in order to present an image endorsed and approved by them. Thereafter follows contentment for *others* because we fit what is expected of us. But, for *self* there exists little contentment. We often feel torn or in conflict as we try to balance personal objectives with societal or group expectations. That is why looking into a mirror and peering deep into our own eyes is so very important. It demands truth.

Did you look long into that mirror, ask yourself honest questions, and give yourself honest responses without averting your eyes? Did you blink excessively or shy away from the mirror and your stare? Did you let your mind become distracted or attend to noise in the environment? Did you think, "Anything—please anything at all—to end this self-inspection"?

FACING THE WORLD

For most of us, facing the world is probably the most difficult thing we do. Depression, anxiety, and panic are not unusual reactions to the pressures associated with interacting with others. Although people are quick to assert their independence and toughness in reference to others, it seems more often the case that we are less independent and assertive than we think. When faced with family, community, and other social pressures—real or imagined—many of us buckle under the weight of possible disapproval. This seems a strange and unlikely phenomenon, given how much trash many of us talk. However, in the arena of social exchange, brashness and bravado can very quickly give way to deference and caution when we are truly pressed to put up or shut up.

Our racial peers often want us to be what *they* want us to be. That is, they are more comfortable with predictability from their "brothers" and "sisters" than with nurturance of individuality. Maintaining your sense of self when blackness is so constantly foisted upon you is sometimes burdensome. Intimidation, guilt, and admonishment traditionally await those of us who choose to expand beyond the limitations of race. But the assumption that a chasm exists between being black and being you is common. What is most compelling is that the chasm is viewed as enormous. However, the new you is not necessarily apart from the black community, but rather an extension of it. The new you is no longer a representative of the black community, but an aspect of its multifarious nature. The new you is no longer part of an advancing vanguard, but one of countless referents on an ever-expanding horizon. The new you is without obligation to role model, mirror, or lead. Your only obligation is to be you and new, intolerant of constrictions from any corner of humanity—even from those corners peopled by individuals of similar skin color.

EMPOWERMENT

Acting as decider of your own fate is an enormous undertaking. It means not waiting on forty acres and a mule, or reparations, or the talented tenth, or food stamps, or Pharaoh to let your people go, or the One, or any other supposed entitlements to save you. Empowerment means being the ultimate voice in your life. Whew! That's a great deal of responsibility to have under your power. And much is riding on that empowerment.

If you manage to do and live well, then it's to your credit. You made the commitments and sacrifices, and you deserve to reap the benefits—no apologies and no modesty, just the fruit of your labor. If, however, you don't do well, then the buck stops squarely at your door. You failed to make the necessary commitments and sacrifices. And guess what? You also deserve to reap the consequences of your poor planning and motivation. Such philosophy carries high costs and benefits. Are you willing to pay the cost to be the boss of your life? In order to do so, you will have to abandon the safety nets and rationalizations of black delayers:

Prejudice
Racism
Discrimination
Legacy of slavery
No leaders

Black advancers not giving back to the community
No father at home
Mother on drugs
Poor schools
Poor opportunities
No jobs
White people
Koreans
Jews
Too few good black men
Emasculating black women
Them putting drugs in the 'hood
Poor role model

Paradoxically, when we let go of these safety nets is exactly when we begin to gain liberation and become free from rationalizations and excuses, free from justifications and pitying benevolence, free from our racial yokes, free from the last vestiges of our oppression. Your slumber of unrealized potential must become uncomfortable. You must become dissatisfied with your present level of development. You must feel some level of anxiety at the prospect of failure. And through that anxiety empower yourself.

FEARLESSNESS—AND A BIT OF AN ATTITUDE

One learns to face the world either with trepidation or with fearlessness. I choose fearlessness for my sake, for my children's sake, and for the sakes of my forebears who had to live terrorized by both their current lives and their destinies.

I am not afraid of the world and my success/failure possibilities because I have always known that with enough hard work, and with enough persever-ance I would succeed. Period! No brag, just fact. My perspective was certainly not arrogance. As a child, I was often told by peers and teachers alike that I was arrogant. When I first heard the charge I was truly shocked and taken aback. I say today, as I said then, that I've never been arrogant—just confident and fearless!

As I matured, I came to see the political connection between arrogance and being "uppity" for a little Negro boy. If people wanted to term it *arrogance*, then so be it. I did not care, and you shouldn't either. "I will be successful," I repeated as a young man while pursuing, with a relentless fervor, my range of possibilities. Success would be mine, without a doubt. Its sentinels—white, black, otherwise—would fall under my spell. To many I am sure I seemed powerless and laughable. But I knew I just had to get in the door. Once in, it was only a matter of time. *They* had already lost the war. The odds were against *them*. I would prevail, just as my black slave forebears had prevailed, given their limited range of possibilities. Presently, our range of possibilities is without limit. Now it is time for you to prevail without limitations from anywhere.

Your successes and your failures are yours. Just incorporating this simple truism into your life will launch you toward success, because you *know* it's on you.

ORIENTATION

Having faced oneself and faced the world, it is now important to concentrate on your orientation to time and history—that is, do you look forward or do you look backward? Do you identify with increasing and unlimited opportunities or do you languish in pools of self pity and limitation based on past history and ego protection? This aspect of the new you is crucial to newness. Without facing forward there can be no transformation—and ultimately no freedom from the limitations of race. Only recounting and wallowing in the past can be attained. Unfortunately, such wallowing has been, for parts of our community, romanticized as some type of noble connection to our history and retention of our heritage. But heritage is based on history—that is, heritage exists in the past. Recounting the past is nice for history lessons, but virtually worthless for lessons in forward movement. Heritage is a footnote, a place from which one launches oneself forward, not backward.

People who know you might initially have difficulty understanding and accepting the new you. That's their problem, not yours. Don't even begin to bother with them. Leave them to themselves and their constrictions. If they care for you and love you, then they will learn to understand and accept you. If not, then move on, beyond them and unencumbered by them. No more conditional love. You are new. New is you. You are different in your outlook, different in your mind, and different in your soul. The new you has the audacity to shout, "It is I and I am strong."

I would suggest beginning your introduction to yourself by getting some extended time alone—perhaps a weekend all by yourself. Kick every damned body out of the house. Everyone, even the dog. Do things that you want to do, have wanted to do forever. Be you. Relish your new self. Believe in yourself. Get yourself motivated and into a frame of mind good for you and conducive of change. Not as black man or black woman, not as a sister or a brother—but only as you.

> I AM FREE: I can do whatever I want.
> I AM FREE: I can be whomever I want.
> I AM FREE: You don't own me.
> I AM FREE: I don't owe you anything.
> I AM FREE: I owe myself.
> I AM FREE!

Nurturance and development of self beyond race has to do with your humanity. What is it that you want to be? Whatever it is, be fearless in its pursuit! What exactly are *they*—particularly black people—going to do if you insist on being you? Will they not speak to you? I doubt it. You can't shut them up now. Will they stop patronizing your business? I doubt it. We are shameless consumers of everything marketable, often without social conscience. Will they make your life difficult? Only if you continue to associate with black losers and delayers, and only if you continue to look to them for approval.

We advancers welcome and support you in your journey. Pursue it relentlessly! When you engage in a nonsanctioned activity, enjoy it. Keep at it. This is nourishment for your new self. When others try to bring you back into the fold—by the way, a term associated with sheep!—remember your journey's end: psychological freedom. Does what *they* are talking about contribute to your freedom or to your constriction? Further, does what *they* are talking about enhance your psychological freedom, or it is simply noise?

You must learn not to fear the new you. Embrace your possibilities for success and failure. The new you looks challengers directly in the eyes and causes them to avert their stares. You succeed not through intimidation, but by fearlessness. You succeed not through guilt, but by excellence. Join other advancers on the road to personal success and psychological freedom, and soon enough you will be in charge of your road. Black advancers characteristically catch, then overtake their role models. Embrace your orientation toward the future. Embrace your new power. Embrace your new you.

The new you represents a rebirthing, a renaissance of humanity lost aboard slave ships. You are you, a self beyond race.

NOTES

CHAPTER 21: GIVE BACK TO THE BLACK COMMUNITY? GIMME A BREAK!

1. Invisibility is a reference to Ralph Ellison's acclaimed novel *Invisible Man*, in which the complexities of black persons are constrained through racism (I say, theirs *and* ours) as well as ideology (again, theirs *and* ours).

CHAPTER 26: THE OTHER SIDE OF THE MOUNTAIN: BLACK IDENTITY BEYOND THE STRUGGLE

1. Although culmination of political freedom is represented in the 1965 Voting Rights Act, several other key judicial decisions signaled being within sight of the summit. These include the first Civil Rights Act (1875), *Brown v. Board of Education*, and adoption of the 13th, 14th, and 15th amendments.

2. Other honorable mentions include conflicts within and between the Nation of Islam and the Southern Christian Leadership Conference.

SUGGESTED READING

Adell, S. *Double Consciousness/Double Bind: Theoretical Issues in Twentieth-Century Black Literature*. Urbana: University of Illinois Press, 1994.

Bush, R. *We Are Not What We Seem: Black Nationalism and Class Struggle in the American Century*. New York: New York University Press, 1999.

Davis, D. S. *Struggle for Freedom: The History of Black Americans*. New York: Harcourt Brace Jovanovich, 1972.

Goleman, D. *Vital Lies, Simple Truths: The Psychology of Self-Deception*. New York: Simon & Schuster, 1985.

Harding, Vincent. *There Is a River: The Black Struggle for Freedom in America*. New York: Harcourt Brace Jovanovich, 1981.

Landrine, Hope, and Elizabeth A. Klonoff. *African-American Acculturation: Deconstructing Race and Reviving Culture*. Thousand Oaks, CA: Sage, 1996.

McWhorter, John H. *Authentically Black: Essays for the Black Silent Majority*. New York: Gotham Books, 2003.

Pollard, J. K. *Self-Parenting: The Complete Guide to Your Inner Conversations*. Malibu, CA: Generic Human Studies, 1987.

Robinson, J. L. *Racism or Attitude? The Ongoing Struggle for Black Liberation and Self-Esteem*. New York: Insight Books, 1995.

Sandler, J., and A. Freud. *The Analysis of Defense: The Ego and the Mechanisms of Defense Revisited*. New York: International Universities Press, 1985.

Part 4

MESSAGES FOR THOSE BEING LEFT BEHIND

We must advance. We must move on. Despite a history of obstacles set to thwart our advancement, it has always been upon us to progress to the next step. Such sentiments have been part of the long history of struggle for black Americans. Now, with virtually no obstacles before us, delayers hesitate. Despite having been shown the road, they insist on not accessing it. In order to continue this journey for psychological freedom, we must detach from delayers and their self-handicaps. We must move beyond them and their dysfunction. These messages and others are the focus of part 4. It has been their choice to adhere to dysfunction. Now, it is their choice to either join us on the road or to be dumped, trapped by the limitations of race.

Chapter 28

WHY YOU'RE BEING DUMPED

Sometimes you've got to let everything go, purge yourself. I did that, I had nothing, but I had my freedom . . . Whatever is bringing you down, get rid of it. Because you'll find that when you're free, your true creativity, your true self comes out.

—TINA TURNER

Nothing is going to be handed to you. You have to make things happen.

—FLORENCE GRIFFITH JOYNER

Although the vignette below is extreme, I believe it captures the essence of what black advancers are facing today. Could we live without the poison, without the dead hand? Many of us have already chosen to do so physically. We've moved out of those neighborhoods, educated our children away from those schools, and oriented ourselves away from the past. Now what's left to do is to cut delayers off emotionally and psychologically—not only cut them off, but also cut out that part of our own psyche that retains and protects them.

The shared history of black Americans is irrelevant. This operation and surgery is an individual decision, not based on guilt, racial allegiance, shared oppression, or any other enmeshing vehicle. We advancers must learn to say to you, our increasingly distant relatives, "You are being dumped because you are

Scene: DOCTOR AND PATIENT
DISCUSSING LABORATORY RESULTS

Doctor: Ms. Johnson, I'm afraid your right hand is gangrenous.

Ms. Johnson: What does that mean?

Doctor: It means the poison will continue to spread through your arm and throughout your body. Potentially, it could affect your heart, brain, and other organs, making them shut down, which would lead to death. Probably in a year or so.

Ms. Johnson (noticeably shaken): Can anything at all be done to stop it?

Doctor: Yes, but some people don't like that alternative.

Ms. Johnson (mildly hopeful): What is it, doctor? What can we do? I want to live.

Doctor: Your hand would have to be amputated. This would stop the spread of the poison. You'd live a perfectly normal and productive life, but without the natural right hand you were born with.

Ms. Johnson (more hopeful): But I'd live and have less pain?

Doctor: Yes. The pain and the suffering would be gone. And you wouldn't have to sacrifice your life to it.

Ms. Johnson (overjoyed): Then let's do it. I can always learn to write left-handed.

a drag upon me. You are actively living the life you have chosen. I now choose to live the life I want. I can support those black persons who are trying to do something positive and not hurting themselves, their families, or their communities. The ones who choose otherwise I cannot and I will not support."

You discredits to the past, present, and future of black people are dead weight—heavy and getting heavier every day. Such burdens cannot be supported long. Carrying you lends credibility to your sloth. Carrying you negates my own struggles. Besides, we advancers are the only ones who seem concerned about your plight. You don't look or seem that unhappy to me, laughing and partying while awaiting arrival of your rescuers. We advancers will continue to unburden ourselves of the weight of the dead and dying. It's liberating. Liberation of individual souls and individual minds, not liberation of the collectivity of black people, is the final step in the journey from enslavement. Black freedom at this phase is absolutely idiosyncratic and personal.

You delayers and discredits are being dumped because you *choose* to languish. As a person who chooses to advance, I cannot become *me* while attending to *you*. I cannot reach *my* goals, *my* potential, and *my* freedom while carrying you through *your* resistance, *your* dysfunction, and *your* sloth. I cannot reach my psychological freedom while addressing your self-defeating behaviors. Your pathology is your own, and so too are your consequences. There are obvious and natural consequences for sloth and delay. I will let you pay the price for your choices. That's just life!

Have you ever felt anger from a relative, friend, or other person because you refused to get off your ass? No matter what they did, what they said, or what resources and time they committed, you remained unchanged. Or worse—you wanted more and resented them for having more than you. Sound familiar at all? Did you feel as if they were trying to drag you—kicking and screaming—into self-sufficiency and responsibility?

I think that perhaps we advancers have cushioned your fall much too much with understanding, rationalization, and defense of your ineffectuality. Perhaps you need to fall—hard and face down onto the cold sidewalk. This is what may be necessary to stir you from your comas. I say comas because truly you are beyond simple sleep. For you do not stir to historical or societal changes. You even fail to react to progressive advances within your own communities. No, for you delayers, coma is the accurate description. You slumber too deeply and too unshakably. And we advancers make it easy for you. On one side your benefactors—family and friends—keep you afloat financially. On the other side, your apologists—do-gooders, race peers, and social programs—bolster you spiritually and psychologically as you sleep.

I have my own struggles and you have yours. I will attend to my struggles and let you attend to yours. Delayers, you must get off your asses and onto the paths laid before you. Actually, they're not paths anymore. That would imply much too small a venue. No, they're roads. Damned near freeways! While you stand on the side of the road with a squeegee hoping to hitch a ride, advancer traffic flows past you—some slow, some at breakneck speed—but it's all moving forward.

Stop making excuses. You know the road's there. And you know how to get on it. The on-ramp is clearly marked. You choose otherwise. Delayers, you must join the traffic or get out of the way. Wake up to the rush or pull over— self-defeated—for a snooze at the No Way Out Inn. Your bed's made. Ready to lie in it?

To all advancers, I whisper, "Shhh! Quiet now—wouldn't want to disturb them."

Dear Distant Relatives,

You're being dumped because you are dead weight. I want to celebrate my life and my achievements. You're celebrating yours. I want to celebrate mine. You've used up your credit with me. I am tired of you and those of your ilk. I have to push on and I will no longer be held up by your weakness. It's on you what becomes of you. If you choose to fall further into your emotional, moti- vational, and psychological abyss, it's up to you. I now and forever release you to yourselves.

Dear Fellow Advancers,

Being free and unencumbered by the weight of others is crucially important in attaining the final phase of psychological freedom. Those who choose *failure* or *waiting* or *the past* are living the lives they want. Dumping them represents celebration of our own lives. Moreover, dumping them represents moving away from community enmeshment, codependency, and dysfunction, and toward psychological freedom. It's time to release ourselves from these racial obligations, these racial roll calls. Time to let go of the anger and the guilt. If you choose to help, then do that. Help, however, is not dependence. And help unrequested or unappreciated is not help. It's enmeshment. Sometimes the harsh realities of life teach their own lessons. If the enormity of the number of people's lives to be discarded is getting you down, forget it. Jettison your guilt and depression. It's hampering you. Do the things you want and let any feelings of guilt dissipate. Letting go of the overinclusiveness of race is one of the central tasks of black freedom. This is important because psychologically we have been mistakenly welded together with all other persons who are black. Through our leadership, media, history, and cultural mythology, we have been clumsily soldered together. Mercifully, the union's dissolving. It was simply ill fitting from the beginning.

Chapter 29

E-MAIL TO A DYING BREED

The first requisite of a good citizen in this republic of ours is that he shall be able and willing to pull his weight.
— THEODORE ROOSEVELT

You don't hold your own in the world by standing on guard, but by attacking and getting well hammered yourself.
— GEORGE BERNARD SHAW

TO: Sister with hair and nails done, but children undone
        Brother on corner drinking beer and holding his crotch
        Sister in the post office with an attitude and wearing pink run-overed bedroom slippers
        Brother on a public bus smoking crack

FROM: JD
RE: YOUR TRIFLIN' ASS

s it me or have you decided to not even attempt to do anything to improve your life? You wake up every day without even thinking about something positive for yourself or your family. You watch television, eat sammiches, and complain of all the things working against you. The white man, the white woman, the Koreans, the Jews, cops, your baby's daddy, your baby's momma—all are in collusion against you, limiting your opportunities and using racism to keep a good brother or sister down.

Actually, you're probably right about one thing. There is prejudice, racism, and discrimination out there. It's alive and rampant. But is that news to you? Of course there's racism. There's *always* been racism. So what? Black people—just like you—have blazed paths for you. Other black people—just like you—have already walked those paths kicking rocks and other obstacles out of the way and smoothing the journey. Still other black people—just like you—have died so you could go to school and have opportunities. And you won't even take your lazy punk-ass down to register for GED or college classes.

You're weak and you're triflin'. I have no use for you. Hopefully you'll not hurt the chances of your offspring. I'm done. You can go back to your pitifulness.

cc: Sister knowing damned well she needs a girdle with them hips
       Brother waiting for a job to come knocking at his—or his momma's—
       door

Chapter 30

LETTER TO
INCARCERATED
BLACK MEN

I could've been a contender. I could've had class and been somebody. Real class. Instead of a bum, let's face it, which is what I am.
—BUDD SCHULBERG (MARLON BRANDO) IN *ON THE WATERFRONT*

It was better to be in a jail where you could bang the walls than in a jail you could not see.
—CARSON MCCULLERS

Dear Incarcerated Black Men,

Since so many of you brothers are rushing off in record numbers to jails and prisons, I thought I'd drop you a line to say hello, encourage you to stay strong, and say thanks. Thank you for the fine brown sisters—from vanilla crème to dark chocolate. Beautiful, luscious, sweet sisters. Small waisted, big-bootie sisters. Thick! And all so very much in need of companionship. Thank you brothers for making it so easy.

It used to be that someone like me would have to rap all day, buy dinners, be nice to the kids, all that. But now, all I got to do is be male. The rest is biology. You feeling me? And I, for one, am not particularly attractive. I'm short and bald, with flat feet and bad skin. But despite these drawbacks, your

251

girlfriends, mothers, wives, and babies' mommas are sweating brothers like me. Throwing themselves at us! And since you're not out there to support them, I and my equally unattractive peers are doing our part to meet their needs. It keeps us busy—Lord knows it keeps us busy! But I just wanted to take some time out to say thank you. With very little effort—and with absolutely no competition to worry about—we've all become players. Your girlfriend, your cellie's wife, even the mother of that youngster down the tier—all them honeys. We don't even have to respect them. We just got to be! Brother, we appreciate your sacrifice. I mean we *really* appreciate it.

I know. We've heard it all before. You love your girlfriend/mother/wife/ baby's momma, and one day you'll be back out there again. Only ten or twenty years to do—3,650 days and a wake-up. But you won't stay out. You'll go back over some other stupid shit and do another ten. Who could blame your girl-friends, mothers, wives, and babies' mommas? Player, you's a drain! Sweating people to put money on your books and accept your expensive-assed collect phone calls. Getting mad when your people don't visit your raggedy ass every week. Trying from behind bars to control a sister who used to be your woman and now belongs to me. And from what I hear, you weren't that good sexually anyway—unless, of course, you've improved during your years locked up.

Anyway, I'll let you go for now. I know you got bid'ness to attend to: com-missary slips to fill out, collect calls to place, gang territories to represent, and institutional counts to make. I just wanted to let you know that you're not for-gotten and to thank you for your women.

Good looking out! I'll holla.

JD

Chapter 31

ENDANGERED SPECIES

Will We Miss the Call of the Wild Homies?

We swim, day by day, on a river of delusions. . . . But life is a sincerity. In lucid intervals we say, "Let there be an entrance for one into realities; I have worn the fool's cap too long."

  —RALPH WALDO EMERSON

Only the paranoid survive.

  —ANDREW GROVE

The 'hood has become so romanticized that much of our nation now accords it special protected status. Not unlike environmentalists attempting to preserve the wetlands across our country, interest groups—race profiteers, carpet baggers, and knee-jerk liberals—stand poised to protect the habitat of the 'hood from those of us who would irresponsibly introduce pollutants into the environment. So lest we put delayers at risk of extinction, contaminants such as accountability, motivation, and self-determination must await the results of environmental impact studies to determine their long-term effects upon the protected habitat and its denizens.[1]

Blind protection of the 'hood because its inhabitants are descendants of a group that was historically disenfranchised is racial blackmail. Many well-intentioned persons are intimidated by the prospect of being labeled racists or

253

Uncle Toms if they suggest that living in the 'hood is to be avoided at all costs. A charge of cultural insensitivity—damned near a felony in some parts—is leveled upon those persons intrepid enough to discuss the misappropriation of the 'hood.

No longer is the 'hood seen as a place from which one need escape, a place where lives and dreams may be crushed prematurely. In fact, the 'hood has been so popularized through music and film as the last refuge for real black persons that many black people who live outside its bounds do so almost apologetically. They speak of how truly fortunate they are to be residing in less dangerous places. (Forgetting that their deliverance from the 'hood was the result of hard work and not good fortune.)

For many, the 'hood has taken on an almost qualifying tone in that residence—present or past—signifies the authenticity of black persons. It reminds me of the theme of a popular credit card commercial. Advancers—no matter how much they've achieved or how acculturated they've become—should never leave home without their 'hood membership card, because, unlike a gas card, it's honored—and likely expected—everywhere.

Despite the desperate protests of race profiteers, beyond the ghetto is where we should be aiming for. It was surely our aim during the Great Migration. And now, with boundless opportunities beckoning, it should surely be our aim during The Advancement. One might ask, "Why *beyond* the 'hood? What's wrong with living *in* the 'hood?" I am always fascinated by such questions, because it seems that in the same breath people are able to lament the 'hood's deleterious effects and also extol its role as foundry of black life.

The 'hood constrains us in our thoughts and deeds. This is the case because in order to maintain a sense of blackness, a limitation must be placed on the range and variability of ourselves. It is not a limitation that is openly advertised or discussed, but it exists nonetheless. Don't believe me? For you inhabitants of the 'hood, count the number of hang gliders, scuba divers, lion tamers, and business executives that live within a few blocks of your home. Very few, if any, right? It's not that black Americans are unable to engage in such activities. It's that such activities are not endorsed as viable means of living or pastime in the 'hood.

Even for those individuals filled with an entrepreneurial spirit, the 'hood provides its own limits. One can progress and extend one's business only so far if being tied to the 'hood is important.

Our 'hoods are our ends. We don't—or won't—see beyond the Avenue or MLK Boulevard. The 'hood has become our security blanket. It has lost its function as stepping stone and is now, in delayer minds, the verifier and purveyor of blackness. Too many of us do not forge out toward unknown but potentially very successful lives. Rather, we remain comfortably underneath our protective blankies—warm and cuddly against each other, shielded from the winds of change. So whether our spheres are nefarious or legitimate, the best that many of us aspire to is to be the top of the bottom—that is, boss pimp or best hair braider, or a variety of other big ballers/shot callers. In our 'hoods is where our delay thrives, and in our 'hoods is where our fullest potential dies.

We must learn to live in the larger world, above the bottom rung. We must learn to be multicultural and multilingual. We must get out of the 'hood. Otherwise we relegate ourselves to the boundaries of the 'hood—all for the sake of staying black.

I am very certain our forebears did not envision that the nightmare of living in the 'hood would one day be viewed in such a positive manner, that its standards would one day be aggrandized by a significant portion of our population. What would they say? We should now be turning away from the ghetto, and toward neighborhoods that are multicultural and multifaceted, as quickly as possible. We should endeavor to become global citizens—expanded far beyond our present bounds—to the suburbs, to the farmlands, to Tokyo, and beyond. As long as the ghetto is viewed as a legitimate place to live, rear children, and educate them, we will be saddled with delayers. There will be people unmotivated to extend their ken beyond what is directly in front of them. And, as a consequence of that shortsightedness, the memories and sacrifices of our forebears will remain distant and unimportant to those who choose simply to survive rather than thrive.

Many will view these writings as disrespectful. Delayers will probably argue that they are not ashamed of where they live and, in fact, are proud of their surroundings. I would counter that if indeed they are not ashamed of their residence, then why complain about its hazards? Why complain of the noise, the crime, the gang thugs, the police thugs, the hookers, the hustlers, the dirty streets, the virulent drug cultures, the pregnant teenagers, the aimlessness, and all the other dangers? Moreover, I would argue vehemently that the pursuit of happiness— not simple and horrifying survival—is what we should be employing as our standard of living. If these words are wrong for you then enjoy your life there and continue partying. Otherwise, join the movement toward psychological freedom. Don't you think we deserve some freedom and respect? I believe many persons still live in the 'hood because they are either unmotivated to move out—feeling threatened by the responsibilities of accountability—or have lost touch with where they are supposed to be looking toward. Why else would anyone live there, let alone defend it?

Scene. SATURDAY AFTERNOON ON DELAY STREET

Charles (standing on his porch sipping on a forty): Where Robert 'nem moving to?

Quincy: Man, Robert and his wife both got hired down at that new factory. I think they moving to Chestnut Hill.

Charles: But why they moving? The 61 bus stops damn near in front of the factory.

Quincy: You know his wife Belinda was always trippin' 'bout the neighborhood. Always said as soon as she could get out she'd be gone. I guess they got enough money to be gone.

Charles: That's messed up. Soon as people get a little something going they move. That's why the 'hood don't never change. Most the good people leave and then more riff-raff move in. Watch. I bet some triflin'-ass folks with snotty-nosed kids move in their place. You watch.

Chapter 32

THE RACE CARD
No Trump

I have struggled against tyranny. I didn't do that in order to substitute one tyranny with another.
—DESMOND TUTU

To the man who is afraid everything rustles.
—SOPHOCLES

With someone who holds nothing but trumps, it is impossible to play cards.
—CHRISTIAN FREIDRICH HEBBEL

stopped playing cards more than twenty years ago, partly because I wasn't very good at it and partly because of the violence and mayhem of the average game. Relatives and friends would play Spades or Hearts, although, if enough true purists were in attendance, Tonk was the preferred game. What I found the most interesting aspect of these games was the rules. Nowhere in the explanation and teaching of the game is the viciousness of its play discussed. Head rubs, comments about a player's parentage, spanking hiney, and laughing while pointing gleefully at vanquished and defeated opponents were common. Episodes of rising from the table to slap down a card with what seemed to me an unreasonable amount of force are not discussed. But such violent episodes are integral parts of the game. At least this was the case in my neighborhood. Who knew such aggression and disdain could be elicited from a card game?

One evening I sat thunderstruck as my grandmother hurled expletives toward my father—her baby boy. Surreptitiously, I picked up the empty card package and searched the small print on its outside. Nowhere—whatsoever— was there a warning detailing the hazards of card play. Given the humbling mayhem that followed each round, a disclaimer should have been displayed prominently on each pack. Something like:

> *The XYZ Card Company, Inc. (hereafter, called The Company) disavows any responsibility for injuries—physical or psychological—sustained when engaged in games involving our product. We advise use of this product only by vicious, stone-hearted, and relatively irrational persons.*

Whether the game is Hearts, Spades, Tonk, or Race, the same aggressive mannerisms are displayed. Whenever I have witnessed playing of the race card, it has been done as aggressively as any other of the games in my neighborhood. And it truly is a game. The object: Try to avoid any reasonable and rational discussion of racial issues after the card hits the board. In most versions of the game, play stops here. Rarely is there any consideration for the opponent or open discussion of the history or intricacies of play. Even rarer is there any attempt to improve the play of the opponent. Worse, witnesses to the playing of the race card often do little toward addressing the unfairness of the situation—other black Americans present at the game know damned well the race card is being played unfairly and only as a defensive move. But they are likely to remain mute—intimidated by fear of being labeled Uncle Toms or sellouts. No understanding and no compassion. Only slapdowns, head rubs, and aspersions cast upon the vanquished opponent are permitted.

It's a rough game, so I don't play. I believe in the dignity of people—all people. I suppose that belief is so strongly entrenched in me because I am painfully aware of the centuries of indignities visited upon my forebears. I have found that directing insults and ridicule toward an opponent is worthless and shameful, particularly without open discussion or the possibility of corrective action. The aggressor—and this is the correct term here—feels better, but the victim feels terrible. It seems our goals regarding race relations should be set far beyond the mere reversal of roles. We should endeavor to do more than have the upper hand.

I would hope black Americans—particularly delayers—would behave in a more civilized fashion and model more humanitarian behaviors. It reminds me of Mahatma Ghandi's and Martin Luther King Jr.'s nonviolent reaction to their aggressors. There is something primitive and base about meeting one's non-aggressive opponent with aggression. It was primitive and base when perpetrated upon us, and it still is. America needs all the allies it can muster in the battle against racism, discrimination, and prejudice. We all know better than to engage in playing the race card. It's just that some people feel so ineffectual in

---

Scene: QUITTING TIME, LOCKER ROOM OF TWM, INC.

Laurie: Ain't this a blip? I got a pink slip in my pay envelope. They lettin' me go. Damn! I know it's 'cause of my supervisor. Racist bitch.

Diane: How you know it was her?

Laurie: Remember 'bout a month ago I got busted a couple of times falling asleep on the line. I told her to put me somewhere else, that I was bored there, but she said I was brand new and had to work up to a better position. Almost everybody over on that other line is white.

Diane: What you talking about? There's blacks and Hispanics over there, too.

Laurie: Yeah, but they were there before she became supervisor. At least that's what I'm gonna say.

Diane: What you gonna do?

Laurie: I'm filing a suit on that white heifer. Discrimination. Racist ass.

Diane: 'Cause she hatin' on you?

Laurie: Naw, fool. 'Cause I'm black. I bet she ain't never promoted nobody black. That's bullshit. We'll see what she got to say when she gets it in her damned mailbox.

their lives that they seek to feel superior in any possible way they can. But make no mistake: The need to feel superior in any way possible serves as platform for racists—no matter what color.

In my opinion, players of the race card are cowards and usurpers of the spirit and sacrifices of others. To pull race in order to trump logic, reason, and rational discussion seems disingenuous at best. It occurs when some weak-minded or weak-positioned person feels bested already and attempts to either level the playing field or to end the discussion. Real competitors, whether involved in a sporting event or a simple debate, do not mind being bested by a better opponent. Beat me with superior knowledge, facts, or presentation. That's fine. But to trump me with an attribute that is all too often irrelevant in the discussion at hand is cowardly. I believe that persons who employ the race card have never been in real competition for any significant prize. They have never prepared and battled hard for any jewel. For if they had, they would know without a doubt that unfairness is unfairness—pure and simple.

It reminds me of competitions during Jim Crow, where the outcomes were already decided by race. For example, think of the farmer who each year looks forward to growing his cash crop of squash. Every harvest, farmers from around the county compete to see who grew the best squash. But there has never been any history of a black farmer winning the Best Squash Award, because the contest is rigged from the very start. The race of the "winner" has been predetermined by the white judges, the white farmers, and, in a larger sense, the white Zeitgeist.

In so many spheres of interaction, black Americans have had those types of experiences. Do we now have the temerity and the audacity to pull the same stuff? Maybe Jamaal Crow is what we should call use of the race card and other such modern behaviors. Perhaps it would remind us how truly unfair the use of the race card is, because it doesn't seem that much different than a white person years ago besting a black opponent as a result of race.

I believe that today's users of the race card are as weak intellectually as their brethren who used Jim Crow years ago to continue subjugation and discrimination toward black Americans. Both Jim and Jamaal operate in the same spirit: to end with an unchallengeable blow the use of logic, reason, rationality, and understanding.

Chapter 33

WHO'S IN YOUR WAY NOW?
Overcoming Yourself

Our goal is to create a beloved community, and this will require a qualitative change in our souls as well as a quantitative change in our lives.
—MARTIN LUTHER KING JR.

A ship in harbor is safe—but that is not what ships are for.
—JOHN A. SHEDD

Black and white persons standing together, arms crossed, swaying left to right—that's how I remember it. Tears welling, voices crescen-doing, "We shall overcome, some day-ay-ay-ay-ay." These are the images I remember from my childhood, operatic scenes repeated almost daily during the civil rights era. The world was very scary during those times, but hopeful. People of all colors had committed to human decency. They had turned to each other for support and strength to face an oppressive history and demand change. And they got that change!

Now the monumental task of turning to overcome ourselves is upon us. So much of who we are has emanated from our epic struggles. For those black persons who remain steeped in the past, it can be very threatening to one's psyche to look around at black progress and consider that the struggle is over—no doubt a terrifying prospect to those who have invested only rhetoric and rationalization toward the future. They must consider that by being remiss, they have been left behind. Black delayers were so busy singing "We Shall Overcome" that few of them considered what would happen once we did— that is, once equal opportunities presented themselves. Equal opportunity, equal entitlements, and equal guarantees meant we could succeed or fail on our own. Many of us have become entitled—thinking we are owed. However, the only ones owed are those who cleared obstacles for us or sacrificed so that we might *advance*. And guess who owes them? Not the white man, the system, or the government, but you and me. We owe them *progress*! Despite the ravings of those who insist that we keep our eyes closed to progress made, *we have overcome*. At least, we have overcome them. Now let's turn to overcoming ourselves.

Initially, when I began writing this chapter, I considered addressing all the things that purportedly thwart us and get in our way. All the things left to overcome. You know, the scam. The one we try to foist upon America whenever our accountability is questioned. We all know the words. C'mon, let's chant them together:

No leaders.
Poor models.
Poor schools.
Street crime.
No leaders.
Poor models.
Poor schools.
Street crime.
Hey, hey, hey!
No leaders.
Poor models.
Poor schools.
Street crime.

But that's all bullshit. I know it and so do you. It really doesn't matter what is in your way. If you want something bad enough, then you'll do what you have to do to get it. Somehow black delayers are able to get those nails done, or that forty purchased, or dem spinners bought. Right? Stop trying to fool white people, the system, your caseworker, your children, your boss, the neighbors, your teachers, me—and yourself. Survey your current position, prioritize your goals, gather your resources, and start stepping forward. If not, then shut the hell up and get out of the way of others stepping forward. Get over yourself. Get over our history. Get over your friends and family. Get on with your life, your future, and the legacy left for you. It's just that simple. I don't want to hear the excuses. You know it's bullshit. But if you still maintain that your excuses are legitimate, then maybe you need to simply accept being one of the ones left behind. If you are already stepping forward, then congratulations. Good for you! Bravo! If others are trying to pull you back, then dump them—undeniably and irrevocably. Dump them, and dump them fast. Once they latch onto you and your dreams, they will mess them up for you. Then what do you have to show for your life? Some lousy, trifling, loser friends with low expectations. Let's compare possibilities: A life filled with opportunities and growth or one infected with rationalization and stagnation. Sounds like an obvious choice to me.

Make a list of your friends, buddies, homies, pod'ners, homegirls, whomever. Are they helping to contribute to your life? Are they, at minimum, respecting your aspirations? If so, then keep them on the list. If not, scratch them off the list, quick, fast, and in a hurry. Stop hanging with them, and stop them from hanging onto you. Why do you keep them as friends? For what? Perhaps to have company as you watch your days, opportunities, and possibilities go by?

Overcoming ourselves is easy. Just think NO!
NO to trifling-ass folks in your life.
NO to lame-ass excuses.
NO to the system's limitations.
NO to prejudice.
NO to discrimination.
NO to racism.
NO to the legacy of slavery.

My life is wonderful because I just think NO. It really is that simple. I have learned not to accept weakness of character from *them*, from *me*, or from *us*. Period. Just as *they* are full of rationalizations and lies, so too are *we*. We must first accept that in many ways *we* are a large part of the problem. The way we think, how we see them, and how we see ourselves all contribute to our self-pity and self defeat. What *they* did in the past and what *they* do now doesn't matter at all. How *we* respond does. What matters greatly is what our ancestors did in the face of seemingly unconquerable obstacles. Accept the fact that black folks sacrificed and died so you could do a little better. That is their gift and it is your legacy. You either choose to accept and honor the gift or not. Stop complaining. It shows your cowardice and simply takes too much energy and wastes too much time.

Overcoming ourselves includes remembering to face forward and step, step, step. Isn't it time for us to immerse our individual selves into the vision of our forebears? Isn't it time to do what those who gave so much could not even dream of doing? Isn't it time to remember where we are supposed to be going: away from The Struggle and toward The Advancement? I'm ready. Are you? If not, then perhaps the central question for you and other delayers is: Are you really disenfranchised—or simply disinterested?

THE DAVISON OVERCOMING PEOPLE ENCUMBERING YOU (DOPEY) SCALE

INSTRUCTIONS: Below appear ten (10) items designed to assess your Overcoming Index (OI). Please answer each item as directly and honestly as possible by circling the response (Strongly Agree, Agree, Undecided, Disagree, or Strongly Disagree) which best fits how you feel about the item.

We could all do so much better if successful blacks gave back to the community.

Strongly Agree   Agree   Undecided   Disagree   Strongly Disagree

Due to this country's history, we black persons are all members of one big family.

Strongly Agree　　Agree　　Undecided　　Disagree　　Strongly Disagree

The United States is one of the most racist places on Earth.

Strongly Agree　　Agree　　Undecided　　Disagree　　Strongly Disagree

If I am able to uplift myself, then I owe it to others to help uplift them.

Strongly Agree　　Agree　　Undecided　　Disagree　　Strongly Disagree

We're just living in the white man's world and subject to his power.

Strongly Agree　　Agree　　Undecided　　Disagree　　Strongly Disagree

White people want to be like us. That's why they tan.

Strongly Agree　　Agree　　Undecided　　Disagree　　Strongly Disagree

None of us are free until all of us are free.

Strongly Agree　　Agree　　Undecided　　Disagree　　Strongly Disagree

They still haven't paid us our forty acres and our mule.

Strongly Agree　　Agree　　Undecided　　Disagree　　Strongly Disagree

If I am stuck, it's more their fault than mine.

Strongly Agree　　Agree　　Undecided　　Disagree　　Strongly Disagree

Generally, the more educated you are the more likely you are to be a sellout.

Strongly Agree　　Agree　　Undecided　　Disagree　　Strongly Disagree

SCORING: A specific point value is assigned to each possible response in the DOPEY scale.

STRONGLY AGREE   = 1 point
AGREE   = 2 points
UNDECIDED   = 3 points
DISAGREE   = 4 points
STRONGLY DISAGREE   = 5 points

Determine your point value for each item, and then sum the points together in order to obtain your Overcoming Index (OI) score. The more points, the more you are overcoming.

SCORE INTERPRETATION:

Total Points
10–20   QUITE DOPEY
21–30   DOPEY
31–40   TEETERING AWFULLY CLOSE TO DOPEY
41–50   NOT AT ALL DOPEY

Chapter 34

BLACK STILL?

Black Selves versus Emancipated Selves

I do not want to die . . . until I have faithfully made the most of my talent and cultivated the seed that was placed in me until the last small twig has grown.
—KATHIE KOLLWITZ

You can love Mozart, Picasso, even play ice hockey, and still be black as the ace of spades.
—HENRY LOUIS GATES JR.

When in the company of other black persons, delayers present a persona consistent with a common perception of what black is supposed to be. They're cool or sullen or boisterous, as the occasion fits. They "girlfriend," "honey child," "brother," and "sister" each other to death. They don their black faces and black facades. Underneath the masks their true souls and individual identities exist, lying dormant and stifled by tradition and community demands. Tragically, for many such individuals, that dormant self is often squashed by misapplied historical references and fueled by fear of ridicule, enmity, and social undesirability. "Keeping it real" serves to keep them real closed and real emotionally underdeveloped. Coupled with psychosocial stressors, such is the formula for mental illness.

Black advancers, on the other hand, choose not to wait for some indeter-

267

minate day of freedom for the totality of black America. Emancipation of self has been, for them, an evolving process for years. They are unmasked, and as a result of being unmasked, they are free to be whatever they desire. Not limited by recalcitrance, anger, or sullenness, black advancers sally forth eagerly, openly embracing new ideas, new relationships, and new ways of being. Their selves are free to develop beyond historical constraints, beyond the community, and beyond blackness. They are free!

This is not solely a black issue. For all humans there exist idiosyncratic disparities between the self we project out to others and the self inside that remains relatively dormant. No one truly gets to know all of who we are. We show others only glimpses of our true selves. This is the nature of being human. But for black delayers, masking is group activity. Masking ratifies induction into their ranks. Sullen, recalcitrant, perhaps even angry, black delayers await a signal for the end of hostilities. No one knows exactly the criteria to be reached, or when or even who will sound the signal, but for them it's coming. Eventually . . . they guess. Only then can they release their sullen selves and progress toward positive growth and development.

In the meantime, they feel justified—nay, entitled—to be recalcitrant, particularly in interactions with nonblack persons. In their minds, to do otherwise is disservice to their enslaved and abused forebears. Their unstated battle cry is: *Every one of our forebears was brought here in chains and as slaves. Until every one of their descendants is free and economically solvent we're standing pat— angry—awaiting our entitlement.*

A case in point from the home front: During my social service agency days, I had occasion to conduct a home visit for one of my adolescent patients. As I entered the poor black neighborhood on Chicago's west side, I was instantly reminded of my own 'hood roots: there existed the same pervasive resignation and the same powerful aimlessness. As I stood on the stoop, to my right I could see the Sears Tower majestically highlighting the skyline. It is truly an incredible sight from that part of the city.

This family had a modest home, purchased by the grandparents six months before the birth of their third daughter, who now stood before me complaining of her son's misbehaviors. As we talked on her stoop—people are sometimes cautious, sometimes ashamed to let strangers into their homes—I expressed how important exposure to new and interesting things would be for her son: a trip to the country, the Greek Festival, a cruise on the lake—whatever.

"Why wait?" I queried Taneesha. "Why not take him to the Sears Tower sometime in the next couple days?"

"You know, you're right," she replied. "That would be good for Marcus to see. I ain't been there yet myself."

How is it possible to live so close to the Sears Tower, see it at least twice every day when exiting and reentering your home, and not venture to visit it? How does one not consider investigating such a dominating part of the skyline? The answers lie in our constrictedness. How often have you heard, "That's white people's stuff" or "Black people don't do that" or "You're thinking/acting/talking like a white person"? People who think that way are constricted, rarely venturing beyond the physical, emotional, and psychological boundaries of the 'hood. Worse, some constricted and delaying persons actually romanticize the 'hood, citing its function as birthplace, foundry, and habitat for black people who are "real."

"If I am me—unconstricted and advancing—who am I?"

"If I am not a 'real black person,' what am I?"

These profound questions are answered: Who and what do you want to be? Now that you've thrown off the constrictedness of *black*, what would you like to be and where would you like your life to take you? Want to be a ballerina? Why not? Want to live with your goldfish in a cabin in Alaska? What are you waiting for? Do you delay because people might think you're strange? Do you wait, hoping that one day you'll get to do exactly what you want to do? Are you stifling and nullifying your dreams, desires, and goals because they are not quite "black enough"? Has the black border patrol beat you down?

Giving in to the beliefs and edicts of others is not healthy psychologically. Forging one's own path and resisting efforts to be subsumed by the views of others are positive movements toward psychological freedom. The world is not black and white. It is not dichotomous. Such thinking is limiting. Black and white, good and bad, brother and Uncle Tom are absolutes and the reflection of constricted lives and minds. Life and its vicissitudes exist in the gray, shaded areas of existence. Absolutes limit use of our cognitive abilities as well as inhibit our ability to grow. A healthy identity—well developed and accommodating—comes from exploration of the grays. Discovering, learning, expanding, and accommodating all represent enhancement of the self. The world is so much bigger than black people, white people, and our history and problems together in the United States. Let's not limit ourselves by these cultural and historical mileposts. They mark the way, but they don't define it. Travel. See different cultures. Learn a different language. Expand. Explore. Grow. Become exactly who you want to be, without apologies and limited only by your own intellectual and motivational potential.

You can forge your own path. You don't need the guidance of your parents, me, Afrocentric philosophies, Rev. Jesse Jackson, Minister Louis Farrakhan, Rev. Al Sharpton, or anyone else. We are not sheep to be guided, shepherded, and reduced to a monolithic convenience. We are individuals—capable of self-will and self-determination. Let our leaders and shepherds pound sand. Do not give allegiance to their agendas unless *you* determine they fit with your own. Black affiliation is little remuneration for the purchase of your soul. Guide yourself to whatever life journey you want. And, in doing so, let others guide themselves. Respect your life and the lives of others. Be who you are and let them be who they are. It's simply not up to you how others turn out, who they date or marry, what they eat, how they act, or what they think.

Becoming is a process that is lifelong. From childhood through adulthood, people have opportunities to learn and expand. If you are essentially the same person today that you were five years ago, then you are likely to be essentially the same person five years from today. Such lack of movement and exploration of the self renders you susceptible to stagnation and constriction. It just makes sense. If you are standing still, you are an easy target for black delayers.

Emancipation of self is the hallmark of black psychological freedom. That part of our psyches that has developed as a result of many years of oppression is one we know quite well. The part that emanates from our own group oppression is new to us. If we were unable to realize our full potential under the oppressive thumb of white society, aren't we similarly hamstrung by black oppression? *They* kept us down in the past, and we fought for centuries to get

out from under *their* dominance. Now *we* keep us down. Are you ready to continue the fight toward the next step of your freedom? It is time to now get *us*
off our backs. We can only realize our absolute fullest potential by getting off
the corners of the 'hood. Whether these corners are physical, emotional, or
psychological is immaterial. We must abandon them.

I refuse to accept the notion that by abandoning the corners we will lose anything substantive. We stand to lose constrictedness, enmeshment, and even codependency. But blackness? I think not. However, an interesting question arises:
How far away from the center of black behavior, attitudes, and philosophy does
a person have to move to be considered *not* black? If I chose to attend a college
that is not traditionally black, am I still black? If I don't like fried chicken, am I
still black? If I marry someone who is white, am I still black? If I believe in ending
affirmative action programs, am I still black? Perhaps more important, if I attend
a traditionally black college, eat fried chicken, marry a black person, and support
affirmative action programs, am I *more* black?

If your answer to these questions is that you're still black no matter what
you do, then why do we castigate those black persons who do such things?
Why do we trip so hard when those black persons exercise free will and self-
determination? What exactly defines whether one is black or not? Who gets to
decide? If, however, you were able to choose one or more of the above behaviors as indicative of nonblackness, then you might want to complete the following inventories.

"Be black," "Stay black," "Think black" all remind me of television and the
film industry. Many of our images of ourselves come from television and other
media. For example, when I interact with black men in the prison or on the
street, I am struck by their cool reserve. Nodding almost imperceptibly their
recognition of each other. Silent. Sullen. Hip. Potentially dangerous.
Remember Linc on *The Mod Squad*? Or, alternatively, they're down for the
cause, too cool to be fooled, and potentially dangerous. Remember *Shaft*, or
how about Hawk from *Spencer for Hire*? For black women: Big bush. Bigger
bootie. Sassy attitude. Remember Foxy Brown? Or, alternatively, smart,
uncompromising, and sexy. Sounds like Cleopatra Jones to me.

If any of this reminds you of you at all, then stop watching so much televi-

STILL BLACK INVENTORY

INSTRUCTIONS: Below appear twenty (20) Yes/No questions designed to assess one's level of blackness. Please circle either YES or NO in response to each item. Respond as honestly as possible in order to accurately measure *your* degree of blackness. Please use each of the twenty items below to complete the following question, "Am I *still* black if I . . . ?"

YES NO   1. Don't live in a black neighborhood.

YES NO   2. Never ate collard greens.

YES NO   3. Attend a white college.

YES NO   4. Believe in ending affirmative action programs.

YES NO   5. Go to the opera.

YES NO   6. Marry a white person.

YES NO   7. Don't dance very well.

YES NO   8. Vote Republican.

YES NO   9. Don't have a big ass (female).
                 Can't play basketball to save my ass (male).

YES NO   10. Listen to classical music.

YES NO   11. Don't like fried chicken.

YES NO   12. Dye my hair blond.

YES NO   13. Have more white than black friends.

YES NO   14. Support gay rights.

YES NO   15. Never refer to black people as brother or sister.

YES NO   16. Don't support reparations.

YES NO   17. Have "conservative" viewpoints.

YES NO   18. Don't love new minstrel shows.

YES NO   19. Don't support the NAACP.

YES NO   20. Don't drink malt liquor.

MO' BLACK INVENTORY

INSTRUCTIONS: Below appear twenty (20) Yes/No questions designed to assess one's level of blackness. Please circle either YES or NO in response to each item. Respond as honestly as possible in order to accurately measure *your* degree of blackness. Please use each of the twenty items below to complete the following question, "Am I *more* black if I . . . ?"

YES NO 1. Live in a black neighborhood.
YES NO 2. Always eat collard greens.
YES NO 3. Attend a black college.
YES NO 4. Support affirmative action programs.
YES NO 5. Go to the club.
YES NO 6. Marry a black person.
YES NO 7. Dance well.
YES NO 8. Vote Democrat.
YES NO 9. Have a big ass (female).
Can play a great game of basketball (male).
YES NO 10. Listen to soul music.
YES NO 11. Love fried chicken.
YES NO 12. Wear my hair in an Afro.
YES NO 13. Have more black than white friends.
YES NO 14. Don't support gay rights.
YES NO 15. Always refer to black people as brother or sister.
YES NO 16. Support reparations.
YES NO 17. Have "liberal" viewpoints.
YES NO 18. Love new minstrel shows.
YES NO 19. Support the NAACP.
YES NO 20. Drink malt liquor.

sion. Develop yourself beyond how others define us. Advance, don't delay. Identify what you want in life. Make a list of seven to ten things, and set out to achieve them all. Even the best of us only get to five or six if we're real lucky. Let those things that are important to *you* guide your life. That's how important they are. Do you want to own your home? Put it on your list. Do you want to visit China? Go for it.

You are you. No one else. It is your life. Don't let entertainers, preachers, race profiteers, parents, friends, or anyone else define you. You are you. Be brave. Be fearless. Be resolute in who you are. And, above all else, be happy.

NOTE

1. The wetlands/'hood analogy may not be a good one because, unlike the wetlands, as far as I can see, the 'hood makes no significant contribution whatsoever to the quality of life for the greater portion of humankind.

SUGGESTED READING

Goulston, M., and P. Goldberg. *Get Out of Your Own Way: Overcoming Self-Defeating Behavior*. New York: Berkley, 1996.

Head, J. *Standing in the Shadows: Understanding and Overcoming Depression in Black Men*. New York: Broadway Books, 2004.

hooks, bell. *We Real Cool: Black Men and Masculinity*. New York: Routledge, 2004.

Horowitz, D. *The Race Card: White Guilt, Black Resentment, and the Assault on Truth and Justice*. Rocklin, CA: ICS Press, 1997.

Hrabowski, F. A. *Overcoming the Odds: Raising Academically Successful African-American Young Women*. New York: Oxford University Press, 2002.

Payne, J. L. *Overcoming Welfare: Expecting More from the Poor—and from Ourselves*. New York: Basic Books, 1998.

Roberts, R. *From the Heart: Seven Rules to Live By*. New York: Hyperion, 2007.

Saltz, G. *Becoming Real: Overcoming the Stories We Tell Ourselves That Hold Us Back*. New York: Riverhead Books, 2004.

Walker, S. *The Freedom Factor: Overcoming the Barriers to Being Yourself*. San Francisco: Harper & Row, 1989.

Williams, Linda. *Playing the Race Card: Melodramas of Black and White from Uncle Tom to O. J. Simpson*. Princeton, NJ: Princeton University Press, 2001.